ADVANTAGE
Business Competition in the New Normal.

By · BILL BURNETT

This book is dedicated to my family.

Without the support of my wife this book

would not have been possible.

For my children, may they build workplaces

where their people are truly engaged and

able to do work that contributes to each

person's definition of self.

TABLE OF CONTENTS

PREFACE

To write a useful book about innovation, one must write a book about problem solving. Lots of innovation experts tackle innovation as though it were alchemy. If you mix a bunch of ingredients into the pot—purple walls, bean-bag chairs, kids' toys, and a foosball table—there'll be a flash of inspiration and *voilà*, the killer innovation will appear! Or rely on good fortune and go into a conference room to brainstorm a solution. Business managers think these techniques are valuable because they do produce a solution. The truth is, you can put any ten reasonably well-educated people in a room, give them a customer problem, and they will create a solution. But if you are looking for competitive advantage, you don't want to settle for just any solution. You want **the** solution.

Included in the book is a road map for creating **the** solution by leveraging the best problem-solving resources within a company. But since this is a book also about innovation, it will first talk about how we create new knowledge. This first section will build a framework for becoming a powerhouse of creating and managing new knowledge. The objective is to make your company that dreaded, fearsome competitor that everyone uses to benchmark the industry. To do that you must repeatedly create competitive advantage by uniquely solving a customer's problem, so that the customer will choose your solution and pay you for it, and your competition cannot copy it. This enables your company to move from innovation to innovation.

Throughout the text are excerpts from the case at the back of the book. These excerpts are there to further clarify points by way of example. While reading the case and examples is not necessary to understand the text, if you chose to read them, you may want to read the case now, or first read the introduction and then the case.

ACKNOWLEDGEMENTS

Albert Einstein

I was inspired to write this book by this little-considered fact: Albert Einstein gave up his position in the patent office in 1909. What is noteworthy about this fact is another fact: in 1905 Einstein published four scientific papers that revolutionized physics. So, what did Einstein do in 1906 and 1907 and 1908? He worked in the patent office. Perhaps this is what caused Einstein to later say: "If at first the idea is not absurd, there is no hope for it."

The physics community is a collection of inquiring, scientific minds. At the most fundamental level, physicists represent the best in intellectual curiosity and integrity.

Yet even this community was slow to recognize the great ideas represented by Einstein's four papers. Much of that failure was due to the mindset around Newtonian physics. Physicists were hampered by their brains' mental ossification around the then accepted view of the world, Newton's view.

Businessmen, on the other hand, are not thought of as needing this same intellectual curiosity and intellectual integrity. In fact, in many businesses, a questioning mind can land you in career purgatory.

Mindset ruins more businesses than any other factor.

INTRODUCTION

Advantage is "any state, circumstance, opportunity, or means especially favorable to success, interest, or any desired end." The question is how do we create advantage in the new normal? The answer is surprising, as we will see.

What does the *new normal* look like? Likely, the engine for global growth will change from U.S. consumption to a broader base of consumption. We will be less highly leveraged going forward. Spending choices will be more thoughtful and the savings rate will rise. What that means to business is simple: competition will be stiffer.

What will not change is basic: the company that owns the best solution to a customer problem will have the competitive advantage. Being good at solving problems is the key to competitive advantage, and that will not change! As humans, we have always marveled at the creative capability we occasionally display, especially when it comes to problem solving. We love it when the solution seems to come out of left field. And, frequently, it is those left-field solutions that deliver that sense of fun in the appreciation of cleverness as in the anecdote told below:

> There is a tale that King Henry IV, the self-proclaimed King of England, decided to impose laws banning displays of ostentation—outlawing pretentious and conspicuous shows of wealth or importance. The regulation prohibited the use of gold and jewelry as ornamentation or part of one's clothing. At first, this law was generally ignored, which irritated the king.

Henry understood problem solving. He didn't put the police in the streets and have them arrest the lords and ladies of the court for wearing jewelry. Instead, he came up with a left-field solution. After giving the vain lords and ladies a period of time to adopt the new regulation, but seeing no significant compliance, Henry enacted an amendment to the law. The amendment exempted pickpockets and prostitutes from the prohibition. The next day, not a jewel or golden ornament was visible on anyone.[1]

King Henry knew how to create advantage. It starts with really understanding your customer and figuring the best way to solve a problem that is consistent with your customer's sense of self-worth.

Henry tried to change a behavior with the tools available to him. Of course, one of the tools at his disposal was enforcement. But enforcement doesn't get to the underlying cause of the behavior. He understood that the lords and ladies wore expensive ornamentation to announce to the world that they were part of the class of important and powerful people. Their clothing was a symbol of their place in the social hierarchy. What Henry did was attack the meaning of that symbol. By linking the wearing of jewelry and ornamentation to prostitutes and pickpockets, he changed its meaning. Instead of signifying importance and power, ornamentation became a statement of crime and immorality. No police action was needed to change behavior. The change in meaning caused a voluntary change in behavior.

Not all people in leadership positions understand how to lead change. The purpose of this book is to help the CEO find ways to

---

1   E. Fuller.2500 Anecdotes for All Occasions, Crown Publishers, Inc. New York, 1942. pp110-111

sculpt the organization without breaking away the good stuff and to create an organization tuned to sustaining competitive advantage.

The other day, I read a blog about creating the successful company. The thrust of what it said was this:

> *The basic requirement for organizational success comes down to a good leader ... The good Leader stays ahead of the curve, looks around corners and knows what is next before it happens. The good leader is a visionary.*

Let's take a look at a leader who fits this description.

THE VISIONARY CEO

Roger Smith, who came up through the ranks at GM to become chairman and CEO, was a visionary. When he took over in 1981, GM was in trouble:

- It had suffered its first loss since its early years.
- The public's perception of GM had been damaged by lawsuits.
- Sour labor relations affected morale.
- Its cars were plagued with persistent quality problems.
- Now foreign competition was cutting into GM's domestic market share.

When Roger Smith looked at the future of GM, he saw a different world. Both industry and market conditions were changing. It was a time when GM still had a strong market position and had tremendous potential to return to its level of dominance of global market share. With that in mind, he implemented massive *out-of-the-box* changes to position the company for this new future:

Automation

When Roger Smith looked into his crystal ball in 1981, he foresaw the importance of robotics in manufacturing. Later that year, recognizing the importance of robotic automation, Smith entered into a joint venture between GM and robot manufacturer Fujitsu-Fanuc. The new company was called GMF Robotics.

Computers

When IBM delivered the first IBM PC that year, Smith anticipated the importance of computers in automotive manufacturing systems. He also recognized that the new microprocessors would enable his industry to put computer-controlled systems in the automobiles themselves. In 1984, he acquired Electronic Data Systems (EDS). Not only would EDS give GM a computer advantage in the automobile industry, but it would provide a second industry in which to grow revenues.

Electronics

If you put computers in automobiles, you need all sorts of other electronic sensors and devices to link to the computers. In 1985, he brought in Hughes Aircraft Company, an electronics powerhouse, and merged it with GM's Delco Electronics as Hughes Electronics. Like EDS, Hughes Electronics would give GM another industry in which to grow revenues.

Cost and Efficiency

Each of the GM subsidiaries and brands operated as independent entities. Seeing redundancy in this independence, in 1981-1982 he reorganized the truck and bus divisions of design, manufacturing, and sales/service into a single new Truck and Bus Group. Then in 1984, he consolidated the autonomous automobile brands like Buick, Cadillac, Chevrolet, Oldsmobile, Pontiac, and Canada cars into just two groups.

In 1982, the U.S. economy was in a recession. Smith used this economy as leverage with his labor force to reduce costs. He was able to cut raises planned for white-collar workers while negotiating wage concessions from the UAW.

Competition

By the early 1980s, Japanese automakers Toyota and Nissan had captured a substantial share of the U.S. small-car market by producing a cheap but high-quality automobile. Smith recognized that in the near term he would be unable to compete on cost and quality in the small market, but he could compete in the next larger size of cars. In 1982, he initiated a program called GM-10 to replace all midsized cars with completely new models across all brands.

When the opportunity to do a joint venture with Toyota appeared, Smith jumped at it. He wanted to learn how the Japanese could build such an inexpensive car with such good quality. Together, Toyota and GM formed the New United Motor Manufacturing Inc., (NUMMI) and located the assembly plant in Fremont California.[2]

---

2   GM announced in July 2009 that as part of its emergence from bankruptcy it will pull out of this joint venture after twenty-five years of success. Toyota announced at the end of August 2009 that in March it will shut down the NUMMI plant. "Today is a sad

Building for the Future

Also in 1985, he launched the Saturn Corporation, a "different kind of car company."

All these initiatives resulted from *outside-the-box* thinking. Robotics, computers, electronics, new models in the right market space, labor and productivity savings, learning the secrets of the competition, and building for the future all seemed like they were right on target. And they probably were.

But Roger Smith failed to achieve the one goal he set for himself—to restore GM to its position of dominance in the automobile industry. He neglected to do the single most important thing a CEO must do. He failed to lead people. He failed to realize what General Wesley Clark realized—that "top leaders can lose by making mistakes, but the winning is done by the troops." The troops don't win by following specific orders. Rather, troops win when they are engaged and empowered to use their skill, cunning, discipline, and motivation to solve problems on the spot.

Likewise, in business, it doesn't matter how well you see the future and set strategy, organize, or try to motivate because the workers do the winning. You enable this capability by engaging the workforce in the battle. Engagement depends on trust and empowerment throughout the workforce. In the end, all of Smith's initiatives failed, some disastrously.

---

day in the history of Fremont as California joins the ranks of states adversely affected by the bankruptcy of General Motors and the worldwide collapse in demand for automobiles," said Gov. Arnold Schwarzenegger.

The 1982 decision to replace all midsized car models was once described as the "biggest catastrophe in American industrial history." Smith was at a loss to explain why it all went wrong, but in the end, GM lost $2,000 on each car produced under the program.

What went wrong was simple. When he took over GM, morale was low, which meant that many employees were not engaged. Employees who are not engaged follow orders and do their work but give nothing more. To turn a company around, you need to create competitive advantage. Solving the customer's problem better and cheaper than the competition creates competitive advantage. Engaged workers will look for ways to do that. They will also look for ways to be more effective and efficient. They want to be part of the solution. Instead of lifting the workforce from *not engaged* to *engaged*, Smith accomplished just the opposite.

When he cut white-collar workers' raises and obtained wage concessions from the UAW, he probably did not do too much damage to engagement. After all, those reductions could be justified. But they were followed by one of the stupidest moves any CEO could make.

Smith announced a generous new bonus program for senior executives. The resulting outrage from the rest of the workforce was so fierce; Smith had to back off the bonus program. But the damage had been done. He took a not engaged workforce and turned them into a disengaged workforce. A disengaged workforce will go through the motions of doing their jobs, but at every opportunity, they will actively sabotage senior management initiatives.

When Smith consolidated the brand companies into two groups a couple of years later in 1984, it disrupted the workforce further. The work on the GM-10 cars fell victim to this confusion and disengagement and never recovered.

It is easy to understand why the robotics program got little support from internal resources. Robots take jobs. What really debilitated the U.S. robotics programs were exaggerated claims about what U.S. robots could do for businesses. Additionally, the installation, configuration, and maintenance of robots required new skills and the GM workforce was not motivated to learn those skills.As it turned out, those early robots proved to be more expensive to install and operate than the manual labor they replaced.

The mythology around these first robots included tales of robots painting each other instead of painting the cars and welding vehicle doors shut. Even though GM was in a joint venture with a Japanese robotics company, in Japan the Japanese continued to make technological advances in robotics that surpassed U.S. capabilities. This had an impact on the product viability of GMF Robotics. By 1986, with falling demand from GM, GMF Robotics cut its workforce to 60 percent of what it had been in 1984.

The EDS purchase resulted in lawsuits, organizational chaos, and bad morale. Moreover, the public dispute between Roger Smith and Ross Perot created great embarrassment for the company. Internally, this seemed more like a personal dispute between two GM executives. Rather than heed Perot's counsel to cut executive perks and streamline the bureaucracy, Roger Smith convinced the GM board-to ante up $750 million to purchase Perot's stock and shut him up.[3] It was easy to see this as the company paying dearly to solve Roger's personal problem. Then it was compounded because the buyout offer was at such a high premium over market that even Ross Perot criticized it.

In the end, GM sold EDS as well as Hughes Electronics. Financially, these were very lucrative deals for GM. But the strategy to leverage these technologies to return GM to its dominant position in the core automotive business failed.

For both EDS and Hughes Electronics under GM's culture, organic innovation did not appear. Both entities grew and expanded their capabilities through acquisition. In any industry, the incremental advance comes predominantly from the internal workforce. A fully engaged workforce will deliver superior competitive advantage far more effectively than an unengaged workforce. Under Roger Smith's ten year reign, GM's workforce was never engaged. As a consequence, GM continued to lose U.S. automobile market share, dropping it from 46 percent to 35 percent.

In the case of Saturn, GM failed to leverage what it learned from the Saturn project. It had been set up independent of the rest of GM, which looked a little like how the brands had been organized before Smith's consolidations. In the end, GM absorbed Saturn, but instead of spreading the value of Saturn into the core GM operation, they transplanted the dogmas of GM into Saturn.

---

3   J. Greenwald, W. McWhirter, J. Szczesny; What Went Wrong? Everything at Once, TIME.com, accessed 11/13/2009, http://www.time.com/time/magazine/article/0,9171, 976990-2,00.html

What Roger Smith did is what many of today's business leaders still do. The manager's first response is "we need to think outside the box." Unfortunately, Roger Smith completely missed the necessary condition to first tap the vast and extraordinary inside-the-box opportunity. If you don't get the inside-the-box capability aligned, then overlaying out-of-the-box initiatives becomes a much bigger gamble. Inside the box is about getting rid of Corporate Kryptonite™[4] and leveraging the enormous (and mostly untapped) talents of your people. In the case of GM, Roger Smith allowed so much Corporate Kryptonite to perpetuate, that none of his initiatives stuck. He never addressed the fundamental issues of T.E.E.™ - Trust, Engagement, Empowerment with the workforce.

The biggest irony for Roger Smith is that the world's best example of inside-the-box value was right under his nose. The joint venture with Toyota was, without a doubt, the single most spectacular example of getting inside the box right. Toyota managed to take GM's worst performing plant and apply Toyota's version of G.O.L.F. T.E.E.™[5] principles to turn it into the best plant in the GM family of assembly plants in less than a year. We tell the NUMMI story elsewhere, but for our purposes here, Roger Smith's goal to understand and leverage how the Japanese built inexpensive, high quality vehicles, was never incorporated into GM.

---

4   Corporate Kryptonite™ is the set of beliefs and behaviors that once were keys to success but, over time, have become obstacles to success. Often, these behaviors are so ingrained into the DNA of the company that the internal people cannot see that they are no longer effective. Corporate Kryptonite™ is a trademark of Dan Wallace and Launchpad Partners.

5   G.O.L.F. T.E.E. is a concept discussed later in the text. It stands for Great Organizational Leaders Facilitate – Trust, Engagement, and Empowerment.

In contrast to Roger Smith's failure to achieve competitive advantage, Robert Galvin, a contemporary of Smith's, focused on the inside-the-box capability and produced extraordinary (and serial) competitive advantage.

THE LEADER CEO

While Roger Smith was CEO of General Motors, Robert Galvin was wrapping up his thirty-year tenure as CEO at Motorola. Today, it is easy to forget what a great company Motorola once was[6]. Under Galvin, Motorola was thriving as a powerhouse of innovation and competitive advantage. During his tenure at the helm of Motorola, sales grew thirty-one fold from $ 217 million to $ 6.7 billion.

Years before Roger Smith faced the competitive challenges from Toyota, Galvin faced a similar challenge in the design and production of color televisions—something Motorola had pioneered. Galvin faced the hard reality, recognized that in the long run Motorola would not remain at the top of the field, and sold the business to the Japanese. He exited in a way that produced the cash needed to pursue new products with better growth potential.

Galvin recognized the Japanese as a long-term threat and saw that they competed on price and quality. Quality was an important element for Motorola and, under his direct leadership, Motorola developed a quality program and named it *Six Sigma*. But under Galvin, the rigors and controls of Six Sigma were balanced by a stronger influence, namely the culture of trust, engagement, and empowerment (T.E.E.™) that fostered problem solving, innovation, and the resulting competitive advantage that generated ongoing strong results.

Galvin's insight into what makes a company succeed as a competitive powerhouse is far different from Mr. Smith's. He understood

---

6   What defines a company over time is its leadership. Companies face their biggest risk when leadership changes.

something very fundamental about building an engine for competitive advantage. It is your internal inside-the-box thinking that matters first. Going outside the box is advantageous and important, but it works only if the internal foundation is willing and able to absorb it.

Galvin focused on what took place inside Motorola. When asked what made Motorola successful, he described it as a set of beliefs and practices that focused on engaging the minds of the collective *we* as he called it, empowering them with support for the development of a very high majority of their ideas, in an environment where truth was paramount. Trust is crucial in an environment of truth. You have to listen for and choose ideas, but you also have to listen for the other point of view. "One of the things that we encouraged was that there would be a more than adequacy of minority reports…we'd go back and say 'Who didn't get heard?' Or 'who got lost from being identified.' Then that gave us another iteration; since maybe we had been too short-sighted."[7]

In addition to *we* being central to their ability to create a "generous share of new products…to be among the first to market these new products," was their approach to risk. "There has been a high spirit of risk and commitment to what needs to be done on the part of the *we's*." To help control the risks around developing new products and technologies, Motorola put in place a process that allowed its scientists and engineers working with other interests in the firm to develop ideas "quicker, better, moved earlier into production, provide better yields."

---

7   Robert Galvin, an oral history conducted in 1993 by William Aspray, IEEE History Center, Rutgers University, New Brunswick, NJ, U.S.A.

And, like all firms that sustain competitive advantage, they maintained a high degree of integrity in all customer dealings.

Galvin relied on the vast, creative, scientific and engineering capability within Motorola to generate the bulk of their ideas. The two key factors of *we* are these: include everyone's ability to solve problems; and foster an appetite for risks. This allowed Motorola to enjoy years of market dominance.

Galvin focused on what took place inside Motorola. Roger Smith did not focus on what took place inside General Motors. Galvin was extraordinarily successful while Roger Smith failed.

Galvin understood that the rigors of quality must imbue the design of products, manufacturing, and processes. Success in delivering quality is dependent on consistency that repetition, control, and focus institute. Quality is guaranteed by a narrow deliberate elimination of variation. Innovation is different. Success in innovation and problem solving depends on exactly the opposite. Innovation and problem solving depend on a completely open resource of many minds that are free to think about problems and opportunities without constraint (at least at first). It is the only way great ideas get traction. Galvin knew how to balance innovation and quality at Motorola.

COMPETITIVE ADVANTAGE

This is a book about becoming *the* competitive powerhouse in your industry. What makes a company a competitive powerhouse is how well it solves a customer problem. You can think of this *customer problem* as a customer's unmet need or desire or want. Whether it is a need or a problem, clearly understanding it is essential to successfully finding something which meets that need, or solves the problem. For our purposes, we will call this need or want or desire the *customer's problem*.

Solving the customer's problems is how companies differentiate themselves. Being better than your competition in the enterprise of problem solving is the key ability. Problem solving is the ability to understand the problem and find the right solution. It is the foundation of innovation. Innovation is a special kind of problem solving. Being proficient at problem solving in innovation makes a company a competitor to be feared. The only impact the new normal will have on companies in the long run is the heightened need to be better at problem solving. Companies that fail to problem solve well will go out of business faster.

Companies come into existence because they can solve some customer problem better than anyone else. These companies enjoy a competitive advantage. Companies go out of business because they fail to solve some customer problem better than anyone else. They've lost their competitive advantage.

Companies innovate to create competitive advantage.

Innovation is not the only way to create competitive advantage. Becoming a monopoly is a good strategy against competition (think utilities). Influencing government officials to choose your company without competitive bidding (think contractor in Iraq) is another way. Become the low-cost or high-quality follower (think fast food company). Compete stupidly and appear to succeed spectacularly just before you crash (think some banks). Or compete on the basis of terror and violence (think the illegal drug business).

Short-term competitive advantage can also be achieved simply by being the first to do something that the competition can subsequently copy. But what we want to talk about is sustaining competitive advantage. To do that, a company must solve the customer's problem better than the competition, and in a way the competition cannot easily copy.

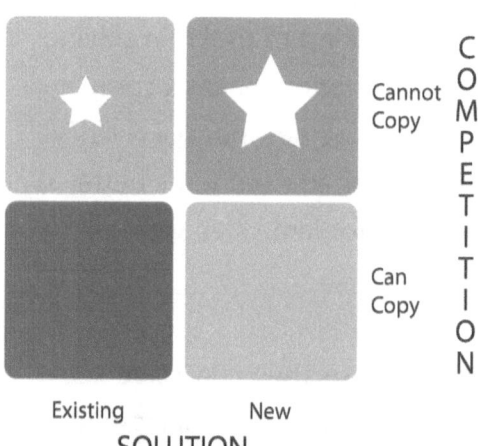

Cannot Copy

Can Copy

Existing   New

SOLUTION

C O M P E T I T I O N

Competitive advantage is found in the upper right corner: A new solution that the competition cannot copy.

Simply put, if you seek a competitive advantage, you'd like a solution to be one the competition cannot copy. The newer the solution the better because every solution has a useful life, and an older solution has less life left in it.

Definition

Innovation satisfies an unmet need in a new way. The *new way* is based on new knowledge, and it is this new knowledge that provides the competitive advantage.

Here, the definition of *innovation* is **creating new knowledge that solves a customer problem and provides competitive advantage**.

Rosabeth Moss Kanter, a professor at Harvard's School of Business, tells an illuminating story:

> *A fabric factory had a long-standing problem of yarn breaking during production. Over the years, the company had explored various paths to fix the problem without success. One morning, a new executive, thinking he might spark the factory workers to start thinking in new ways, called them together and asked if anyone could come up with an idea to fix the problem. Hours later, an older worker who'd been in the factory for a long time, approached him with a suggestion. It worked! A few days later, thinking he'd sparked this moment of inspiration, the executive asked the worker when he had come up with the idea. "Thirty-two years ago," he answered.*

This story is told to show that innovation isn't only about new products; it can be valuable in operations, marketing, etc. It is also used to point out the value of creating a culture in which ideas can be brought forward by any problem solver in the company.

Interestingly, this fabric company would have been better off had the worker initially gone to a more innovation-friendly company with the same problem. Let's assume this other company had implemented this solution thirty-two years ago and protected it with a patent. About halfway through the thirty-two years, the patent would have expired, and any company with the yarn-breaking problem could then have implemented the solution. Thus, the company in the story would have had access to the solution many years earlier.

I like to use this story for another reason altogether because it really isn't a story about innovation at all. It's a story about problem solving. The company didn't really need an innovative solution. It wasn't looking for a competitive advantage, per se, the factory just needed a solution to the yarn-breaking problem. In that sense, everyone would have been happy to take someone else's solution and apply it to the problem. The story underlines the notion that problem solving ability is key to every aspect of change in a business.

However, when competitive advantage drives the change effort, then we are looking for new knowledge. We can end up with two kinds of new knowledge:
- Knowledge that is eligible for Intellectual Property protection.
- Knowledge that is not eligible for protection (know-how).

If the new knowledge is simply know-how, then the advantage may be short lived. If the new knowledge can be protected, e.g., by intellectual property law, then it may be enjoyed for a longer time. But sooner or later, a different innovation will be needed.

Innovation requires new knowledge. Protecting that intellectual property helps sustain competitive advantage.

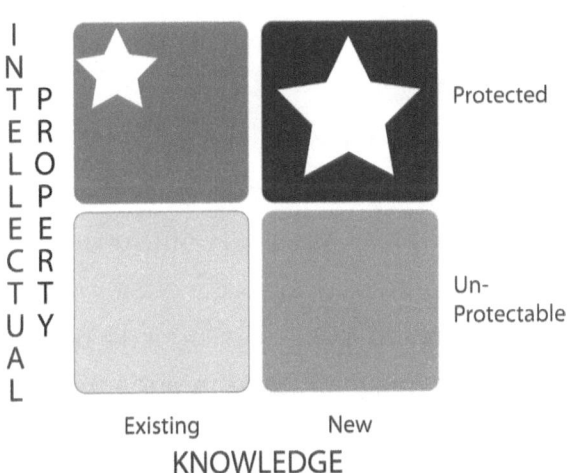

Companies strive to create competitive advantage based on new knowledge that can be protected. They will either use intellectual property (IP) law to accomplish that or create an internal mandate to keep the knowledge away from the competition.

Brachiating Innovation

What determines the need for a different innovation often isn't the company's ability to protect its knowledge. What determines the need for a different innovation usually is a change in the customer and a mutating customer problem.

To survive the long haul, companies must progress from innovation to innovation, product to product, structure to structure, business model to business model much as a gibbon monkey swings from branch to branch through the jungle. A successful company never depends on one innovation to sustain it for a long period of time. What endures over time is the company not a particular innovation.

The ability to problem solve and the ability to create new knowledge are key.

Chicken or Egg

When we talk about innovation, we envision first defining the problem and then finding the solution. Masking tape was developed when painting cars with two different colors was popular. Unfortunately, the two colors would often bleed together as the second color was added. To solve the problem, 3M invented a glue that formed a tight seal but could be removed without damaging the paint underneath the tape.

Masking tape allowed the painter to apply two colors without one bleeding into the other.

In the case of masking tape, the painter had a problem, and 3M found a solution. Problem first – solution second.

However, sometimes we don't start with a problem. Sometimes we innovate by creating a solution, and then we go find a problem. When Dr. Spencer Silver came up with a glue that stuck well to one surface, but when dry would barely stick to the other surface, it wasn't regarded as much of a success by 3M. It was a glue that didn't work well. However, it turned out to be a solution to an undiscovered problem. Four years after Dr. Silver announced the glue, Art Fry was in church singing hymns and losing his place in the hymnal. He spent the next six years applying Silver's glue to develop a hymnal bookmark. We all use that bookmark today—more commonly known as a Post-It° Note.

In this case, 3M had a solution first and then found the problem.

Blue Sky Innovation

Another way new knowledge can be intentionally created comes from pure brainstorming. This is blue-sky thinking, which starts with the goal of creating new knowledge. Intellectual Ventures is a company that brings together extraordinary minds to engage in blue-sky thinking. They start out with a theme, topic, or area of interest and let the conversation go wherever it wanders. Often, the conversation drifts far afield of the original course. This produces some extraordinary ideas that Intellectual Ventures will patent and later license. The individual ideas can come from a discussion of a problem or a discussion of some scientific investigation and often involve the combination of knowledge from different participants to create something entirely new.

Regardless of where or how the knowledge is created, for an innovation to be successful, including a blue-sky innovation, **it must solve a problem better than competing methods**. (And, of course, buyers need to be willing to pay for it.)

Sometimes, inventors become married to the cleverness of their invention and then try to find the right problem to address. Lots of these kinds of blue-sky ideas fail because the problem is defined to fit the solution not the other way around. Take the creative cleverness of the LG Internet Refrigerator.

> *The LG Internet Refrigerator is a stainless-steel, side by side refrigerator. It features a built-in computer with a touch-screen LCD monitor mounted on the door. You can watch TV, listen to music, take and store photos, make a phone call, surf the Internet or use it as a message board.* [8]

What problem did LG think it was solving with this product? "Gee, I am having a hard time keeping the children occupied while they sit in front of the refrigerator...Ah, what I need is a refrigerator that plays TV!"

The key to successful blue-sky innovation, or any innovation for that matter, is to be able to define problems properly and create the new knowledge that best solves the problem.

---

8   M. Hanlon, LG Internet Refridgerator, Gizmag.com, accessed 11/13/2009, http://www.gizmag.com/go/1132/

Innovation as a Side Effect

A colleague suggested that we have situations where industry participants get together to innovate without seeking a competitive advantage. Everyone joins forces to find a solution to a common problem. An example is the payments industry. It gets together to establish standards for things like what information is stored in the magnetic stripe on the back of a credit card. I asked whether it mattered if the solution was based on new knowledge or could it employ something that already exists but perhaps in another environment? The answer is that "it simply must solve the problem." It does not have to be innovative, although it often can be.

In this circumstance, what is needed is a solution to a problem. There's no need to create new knowledge because competitive advantage is not a necessary condition of the problem. Existing solutions can be employed, as long as they solve the problem. This is the distinction between normal problem solving and innovation. In this case, what was needed was a solution to the problem. The business was not seeking competitive advantage. In this circumstance the solution may be the result of new knowledge, and thus innovative in that respect. But the newness of the knowledge is a by-product not a key objective. See below:

In the case at the back of the book, the business driver for solving the losses problem did not have competitive advantage as an important aspect. While you could argue that any change to the cost structure of the business affects the company's competitive advantage, in the case, this was not explicit. In fact, the solution did not need to be inventive at all.

When Bobby Brinkman reorganized the work and changed the way the department measured performance, his solution happened to be quite inventive. But his purpose was not to create new knowledge or to be innovative. He just wanted to eliminate losses.

The old process distributed chargeback cases to the clerks in a way that permitted the clerks to own only the cases on which they chose to work. Because they were measured on the number of cases completed every day, their incentive was to complete as many cases as they could that day. However, in document chargebacks, it was rare for a clerk to work through the entire stack of cases he received each morning. The stack often represented several days of work. Since each clerk received a random stack of cases each morning, clerks would rarely see the same unworked case on two consecutive days.

To maximize the number of completed cases each day, clerks would go through the stack of cases each morning, identify the easiest cases, and focus on those. At the end of the day, the difficult cases would still be in the unworked pile, so they would be returned to the pool of cases for random distribution the next day. Since chargebacks are perishable, the more difficult cases could go unworked right up to their expiration date.

Bobby reorganized the work so that each clerk was assigned a particular chargeback reason, making all the cases within a reason code the responsibility of one clerk. That eliminated the clerk's ability to cull the more difficult cases. The clerks were measured on keeping their inventory free of losses and were given production credit for every case closed within the time frame for that reason code.

But that wasn't the part of the solution that was inventive. What made it inventive was how the department allowed clerks to get incremental productivity. If a clerk felt his desk was up-to-date, he could help another clerk with the cases on that desk. Every case that clerk completed on the other desk would increase his productivity. Since the owner of the desk also got credit for the work, the owner was happy for the help.

Clerks learned how to game the system by switching desks and getting double credit fairly quickly. This is precisely what Bobby wanted to occur. It meant the inventory would be current. It caused people to learn to trust each other with their inventory and built a sense of teamwork. It also created a natural backup capability that was useful when people went out sick or on vacation. The solution was inventive but not innovative since it wasn't about competitive advantage.

The business effect was spectacular because it eliminated chargeback losses completely.

Companies sometimes develop a *Not-Invented-Here* mindset. In this mindset, people inside the company show a persistent unwillingness to adopt an idea or product created elsewhere. Clearly, where a company is solving a problem where competitive advantage is not at stake, this mindset is a handicap. But it turns out, that even where competitive advantage is the goal, this mindset can work against you.

There is an alternative to creating new knowledge yourself. This is often referred to as *open innovation*. Proctor and Gamble use this method extensively. They go out and find someone else who has created a new solution and purchase that knowledge.

In history there are lots of examples of businesses obtaining new knowledge from the outside. Most of the time, the businesses will use an above-board method for obtaining this new knowledge. But not always as we will below:

Joseph Henry, a schoolteacher of young boys up in Albany, New York, was the inventor of the electromagnetic telegraph in the United States. He used the construction of electromagnet as a way to engage the boys. Originally, he had his schoolboys create mighty electromagnets by wrapping a lot of wire around a chunk of iron. Eventually they built one that would lift 1,500 pounds.

They took great pleasure in lifting several blacksmith's anvils at a time, then disconnecting the battery, and letting the anvils crash loudly to the ground. Joseph Henry realized that he could string wires over great distances and cause the same thing to happen. For Henry, the fact that this method could create a sound triggered the idea that the method could be used to communicate. Eventually he built a small device that emitted a click.

That is basically how a telegraph works. An electromagnet gets a jolt of electricity, this causes two pieces of metal to quickly come together with induced magnetism, and the contact makes a clicking sound. Later, Henry strung wire around Princeton University for a working telegraph. Later still, in 1838, he received a visit from an interested fellow named Samuel Morse, who dashed back to New York and subsequently patented this technology. Joseph Henry believed that such a useful technology should be available to everyone and hadn't pursued a patent.

Regular Problem Solving

It is perfectly legitimate to solve a problem without being innovative or without creating new knowledge. In fact, most problems are solved using existing knowledge in practiced ways. In Kanter's story about yarn breaking, it really didn't matter if the solution was innovative, as long as it solved the problem. However, when it comes to competitive advantage, being good at creating new knowledge in problem solving is crucial. New knowledge is essential to innovation.

Whether innovation is needed or just a solution to a problem, the same fundamental skill is required—the skill of problem solving.

Talent

Problem solving is a talent, and like other human talents, some people are extraordinarily good at it. Through stories, we will explore how we create new knowledge and gain an understanding of why the mix of talents associated with being a successful leader in business is not the same mix of talents needed to be successful at creating new knowledge. Getting the right humans engaged to create new knowledge is the keystone to problem-solving, innovation, and meeting customer needs better than the competition.

Our ability to define and solve problems is what separates us from everything else in the known universe. But this incredible mental ability comes with its own set of limitations. Companies that understand these limitations and develop strategies to overcome them, stand a better chance of creating extraordinary solutions. This book will explore those strategies. Fundamentally, this book is about new knowledge and problem solving as the most powerful mechanisms for competitive advantage.

KNOWLEDGE

New knowledge is the foundation of competitive advantage.

The key to creating that advantage—which is important any time and critical to survival in a tight economy—is to develop knowledge that your industry rivals do not have. We call this *unique new knowledge*. This knowledge will place you on the path of least resistance while leaving the competition on a path of more resistance.

Examples of unique new knowledge include:

- Intellectual property protected by a company's copyrights, trademarks, and patents;
- Tacit knowledge developed within the firm by its employees and used to deliver the company's product or service; and
- Combinations of public knowledge used in the firm that is not currently exploited by the competition, even though the information is available to them.

Unique new knowledge is the firm's most valuable resource. Computers store information. People store knowledge individually, and more powerfully, collectively. People are also the sole source of knowledge, which is why a smart firm's most prized asset is its people. This includes the machine operator on the factory floor who knows all the quirks of the machinery, the chemist who knows how to formulate the product's ingredients, or the manager who is redesigning a delivery process.[9]

---

9   The difference between information (data) and knowledge is that you can store information in all kinds of media. But knowledge resides only in human brains.

In the case at the back of the book, Bobby Brinkman was able to place the redundant chargeback workers elsewhere in the bank by using knowledge as their advantage.

This was not about creating unique knowledge, except in the sense that nobody else in the back office had this level of knowledge. The knowledge itself wasn't innovative—but the training Bobby put everyone through was. By creating a computer-based test that pulled a random twenty-five multiple-choice questions from a pool of 100 questions, he made passing the test a matter of being able to find information in the association's manual.

His goal for employees was to enable them to perform expertly in the chargeback department. But he also educated them with the objective of making the workers more desirable to other departments.

By training them to be experts in the association manual, they developed a superior level of knowledge about the business. This made these employees more valuable to other departments in the back office. Bobby placed no restriction on any employee who had an opportunity to move to a different department in the back office. Occasionally he did talk to his workers when he thought the offer they were considering wasn't good enough.

In the end, he lost some of his best workers, but his faith in all the workers paid off since everyone who happened to remain in chargebacks performed well.

Bobby avoided laying off anyone because this internal advantage made the chargeback people more valuable to the business.

Innovation Is New Knowledge

Innovation is the activity of producing new knowledge to solve a customer problem and provide competitive advantage. The objective is competitive advantage. Competitive advantage is obtained by creating new knowledge. The new knowledge must be an *on-target* solution to the customer problem. To be such a solution, the first, most critical action is to *get* the customer problem right.

In this section, we are going to explore how this knowledge is created. By understanding how we create knowledge and who creates it, we can help a company become the envy of the industry.

In 1963, when I was a boy of twelve, my father took me down to the pipeline terminus south of Sidon, about thirty miles south of Beirut, Lebanon. Tapline, the company for which my father worked, was about to do something no pipeline company had ever done.

The company was eager to install a new thirty-six-inch diameter pipeline from the shore to a berthing spot for tankers out about two kilometers into the Mediterranean Sea. This new line would more than double the throughput of the existing line. However, constructing this large pipeline under water was difficult and expensive—not to mention dangerous.

Oil pipelines take a great deal of pressure, and the welds that hold the pipe together must be flawless. Keeping a section of pipe in place against undersea currents and over bumpy undersea terrain adds to the difficulty of underwater welding.

My father came up with a very simple answer: build the pipeline on land, float it out to sea, and sink it in just the right spot.

This was actually not a new idea, but the company was hesitant because it had not worked well in the past. Sinking a large pipeline was not as simple as it sounded.

It turns out that when you go to sink a pipeline, you must replace the air in the pipe with water. Water flows downhill, so as a wave swell on the surface causes the pipe to flex, the water will go to the lowest point on that flex and start to collect. As the water collects, that portion of the pipe starts to sink and collect more water. Air can get trapped between these pockets of sunken pipe causing sections of pipe to rise. As the pipe sinks unevenly, when it settles on the seabed, this unevenness causes permanent bends in the line. These bends in the pipe can weaken it.

The company had experience with these problems, as they'd already sunk a handful of pipelines at the Sidon terminal. The greater diameter of a thirty-six-inch line increased the challenge.

My father was a great problem solver and loved challenges like this. For him, the more elegant the solution, the better. He thought long and hard and found a way to sink the pipeline. Once the floating line was in place, the cap on the shore and was cut off and a specially prepared section of pipe was welded on. In the special section were three thirty-six-inch diameter rubber balls that were filled with water. The first ball was inserted into the pipeline, followed by fifteen feet of fresh water. A second ball went in after the water. Next gasoline was pumped in filling about 1,000 feet of pipe. The third ball followed the gasoline, and behind that, seawater was pumped in gradually to push the three balls along. The positive pressure against the leading ball prevented the air in front of it from leaking backward and creating the dreaded air pockets.

By avoiding the formation of air pockets, they eliminated the subsequent uncontrolled buoyancy problems. The gasoline, which is lighter than seawater, allowed the pipe to be gradually and evenly submerged, starting from the beach and ending at the ship berthing point. The pipe endured only minor stresses, which ensured that the line was undamaged and ended up where it was intended.

I began to wonder why my father was able to solve these kinds of problems when others could not. My father certainly had good education credentials. He held a BS in electrical engineering from U.C. Berkeley and an MS in mechanical engineering from Columbia. Plus, he'd already published and presented papers in his field as an inventive pipeline engineer. But he was hardly the sole expert in Tapline. Several engineers had similar credentials, and most had more experience. In fact, my father often referred to one of them, A.E. Olson, as the best engineer he'd ever met. Dad called him a genius.

After watching my father work, I knew that the ability to create unique knowledge played a key role in his ability to solve problems. Obviously, knowledge alone was not sufficient to find the great solution. Something else was at work in my father's brain.

A year or two before Tapline successfully sank the pipeline, for Christmas I received an air-pump gun that shot ping-pong balls. This was a very disappointing gift because I'd been lobbying for a pellet gun to shoot birds. However, my mother, worried I'd shoot out my eye with the pellets, bought a ping-pong ball burp gun. It consisted of a clear plastic tube and a hand pump. You built up pressure and then released the air to propel the ping-pong ball out the end of the tube. No birds were in danger from this gun. It barely propelled the ping-pong ball across our living room.

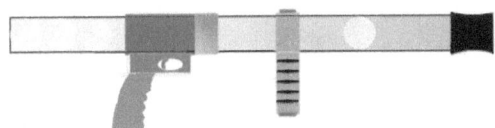

The Burp Gun.

It turns out that it amused my father more than me. A couple of days following Christmas, my father picked up this toy and began experimenting. He held one hand over the open end and allowed changes in pressure in the tube to move the ball along. Thinking back on watching my father sitting on the couch, playing with the ping-pong balls in the tube, I wondered if his mind later used that as a metaphor for his pipeline solution. Years later, when I asked, he thought it was very possible that, in the back of his mind, the fact that the ping-pong balls held a pocket of pressure in the tube may have led to the pipeline solution.

Synthesizing Knowledge

This kind of thinking—that takes knowledge from one area and applies it in a new way—is called *synthesis*. Everyone does this. It's what defines us as human. My wife does it almost every time she cooks—always to the delight of my taste buds. This drive for change seems particularly human. When you think about change in the universe, things like fusion, fission, gravitation, electromagnetism, mutation, evolution come to mind. But only humans innovate. As intelligent as dolphins are, they haven't figured out how to fly or to live outside water.

Flying Dolphins

We've figured out ways to stay underwater longer, dive deeper, and make things that go faster through water[10] than dolphins.

10 Dolphins can swim very fast. Dall's porpoise can swim on or near the surface at speeds reaching 55 mph. While we have surface boats that travel faster—underwater,

Granted, we're not as quick and agile as they are underwater. But, chances are that someday, someone will build a robot that will catch fish underwater with more speed, agility, and better technique than a dolphin. We can easily believe that such a device would be possible to build today!

Monkeys

My daughter, who is studying zoology, pointed out to me that monkeys have developed tools. They've been observed using a stick to dig out termites from a termite mound. Even more interesting, Masao Kawai noted that a Japanese monkey named Imo (the monkey didn't actually call herself *Imo*) discovered that she could separate wheat grains from sand by tossing the mixture into water. The wheat floats while the sand sinks. Other monkeys in the colony subsequently picked up this invention. Okay, that's inventive, and we could allow that it is also innovative if it intentionally gives the monkeys in that colony a competitive advantage. However, I don't believe competition was on Imo's mind at the time of the discovery. Do monkeys have minds? I think so. Once, when I was a boy, we were visiting the London Zoo, and at the orangutan cage, some young men were mimicking the apes, jumping up and down, screeching and scratching themselves. They were clearly trying to torment the animals. Suddenly, a large male orangutan sprang up the bars at the front of the cage, looked down at the young men, and peed all over them. I think he had something on his mind. Earl Miller, who directs research at the Picower Institute for

the fastest submarine is the Soviet Papa class submarine achieved a top speed of 44.7 knots (82.8 km/h). In 2006, Iran claimed the fastest underwater vehicle, a missile that could travel 233mph (360km/h).

Learning and Memory at the Massachusetts Institute of Technology (MIT), on the neural mechanisms of attention, learning, and memory, has done some fascinating work with monkeys and has shown that they are able to restructure knowledge and see something in a new way.

But, perhaps humans have a huge advantage over monkeys. Not only do we synthesize better, but we have a level of complex language that allows us to transfer knowledge to one another. Additionally, we are capable of storing information outside our brains for others to access. Perhaps this storing and sharing knowledge is more than a capability; it might be a human need.

Synthesis is high-level thinking. It leverages existing knowledge in the brain. The invention of separating wheat from sand was the result of discovery not synthesis.

We have three principal mechanisms for creating new knowledge and finding innovative solutions: discovery, experimentation, and synthesis. We will briefly talk about all three.

DISCOVERY

Discovery, the first of three methods for creating new knowledge.

Sir Isaac Newton said, "If I have made any valuable discoveries, it has been owing more to patient attention than to any other talent." Discovery is born of paying attention.

One day in ancient Egypt, Amal is walking along the muddy bank of the Nile and sees the imprint in the mud made by a giant crocodile. In the imprint are some crushed reeds that are criss-crossed and matted, and the mud collected in the reeds bears the impression of the crocodile's patterned skin. He picks the reeds up and notices that they're stuck together and have formed a flat surface. He says to himself, "Hey, I could make some silver coins selling this. But I don't want people to realize what it's made of, so I won't call it papyrus. So what should I call it…ummm….Ah ha! I'll call it *paper*."

Discovery is usually serendipitous. Somebody stumbles across something and recognizes its commercial or scientific value. There is also *directed discovery*. Edison once sent explorers to South America and Asia on discovery missions. They were after a specific texture of plant material that Edison thought would make the best light filament. This was directed discovery. This notion of going out into the world to discover new knowledge is not often used anymore. But it does happen. Landing robots on Mars, for example, is directed discovery in the sense that we are looking for signs of water and perhaps evidence of life.

Charcoal had to be discovered. Charcoal is simply wood that is burned in an environment lacking enough oxygen to complete combustion. When enough air is available, combustion is complete, and all you're left with is ash. Without enough oxygen, the temperature does not rise as easily, and the lower heat drives out resident moisture, organic compounds, and chemicals in the wood, leaving just the carbon. In wood, the moisture and other combustibles burn at a lower temperature than does carbon. This means that you can burn away these other parts of wood at a temperature at which carbon does not combust. Carbon burns hot. It burns so hot that, in a forced-air furnace, charcoal will melt metals. It is this ability to produce higher temperature that has made charcoal valuable.

If you ever wonder whether science or technology came first, think of charcoal. People have used the greater heat produced by charcoal for thousands of years longer than we've known the science behind charcoal. Technology came first in this case.

The second method of creating new knowledge is experimentation.

EXPERIMENTATION

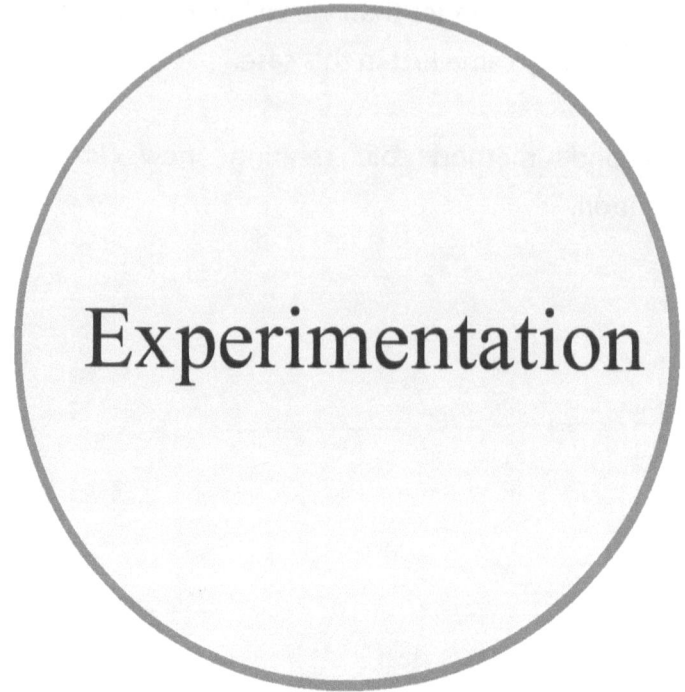

Experimentation

Experimentation is the second way we create new knowledge

To go from discovering some charcoal at the bottom of a fire, to making it in sufficient quantities to sell, required finding a better process. This was done through experimentation. Different solutions were tried, and some worked and others didn't. Around the world, the successful solutions were identical in key respects and different in others. In some places, pits were filled with wood, covered with earth, and the wood allowed to burn slowly for a while. The flow of oxygen to the fire was limited and at the right point, it was shut off entirely. In other places a mound of wood the size of a one-story house would be covered with leaves and dirt and allowed to burn while the air flow was controlled. In still other places, great kilns were built that allowed precise control over the burn process.

All solutions controlled the timing and amount of oxygen available to the fire, which allowed the heat to build up to around 260 degrees Celsius and the air to be cut off entirely at the end of the process. Experimentation also taught charcoal makers not to mix soft and hardwoods, that hardwoods make better charcoal, and that some by-products, such as turpentine, could be recovered and had value.

Sometimes experimentation turns into discovery.

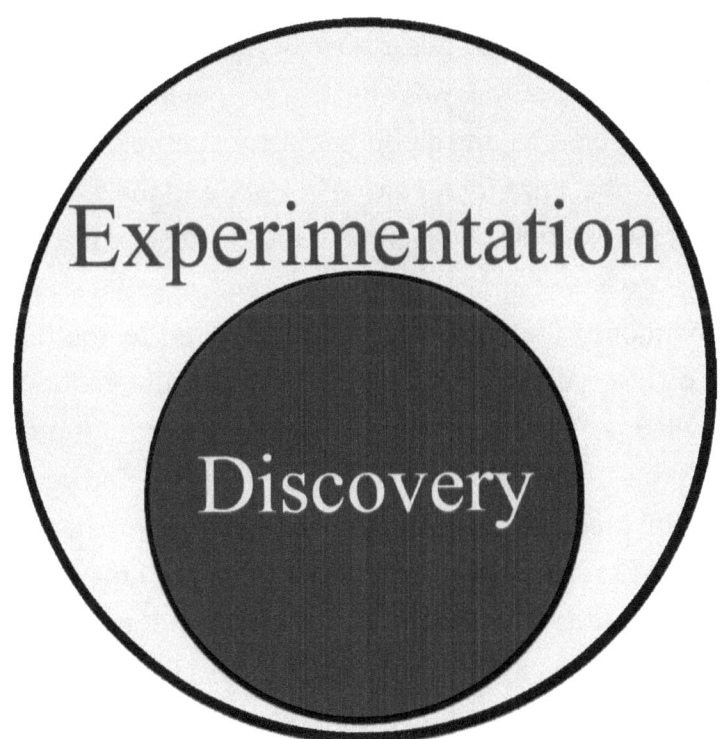

Experimentation leading to Discovery.

In 1928, Alexander Fleming was conducting experiments in a search for a cure for typhoid. Like many innovative people, his approach was often more expedient than careful, and he wasn't very rigorous with proper laboratory technique. His lab was often in chaos. So, when he decided to leave on a long vacation, he left things as they were, including experiments in progress. Upon his return, he found most of his culture dishes had become contaminated with a fungus and tossed them into a sink filled with disinfectant. Later in the day, when a visitor appeared, Fleming pulled out a culture dish that had not been submerged in the disinfectant to show his visitor the fungus. When he did, he noticed a border around the fungus where the cultured bacteria seemed unable to grow.

Of course, we all know this is how Sir Alexander Fleming discovered penicillin. Ironically, it was effective on meningitis, scarlet fever, gonorrhea, pneumonia, and diphtheria but not typhoid. Nevertheless, he won the Nobel Prize for Medicine in 1945, and the story provides us with a good example of experimentation leading to discovery.

We mentioned that Edison once sent explorers to South America and Asia on discovery missions. He also used Experimentation to gain new knowledge. "It has been said of me that my methods are empirical. That is true only so far as chemistry is concerned. Did you ever realize that [in] practically all industrial chemistry...comparatively little [knowledge] has been really settled." He went on. "I may make hundreds or thousands of experiments out of which there may be one that promises results in the right direction. This I follow up to its legitimate conclusion, discarding the others, and usually get what I am after. There is no doubt about this being empirical; but when it comes to problems of a mechanical nature, I want to tell you that all I've ever tackled and solved have been done by hard, logical thinking."[11]

I think all of us, at one point or another use discovery and experimentation to increase our knowledge.

We've already talked a bit about the third method that we use to create new knowledge and innovate—synthesis. This is what Edison meant by "hard, logical thinking."

11 F.L. Dyer and T.C. Martin, *Edison: His Life and Inventions*, (New York: Harper & Brothers Publishers, 1910), 300-301.

Synthesis

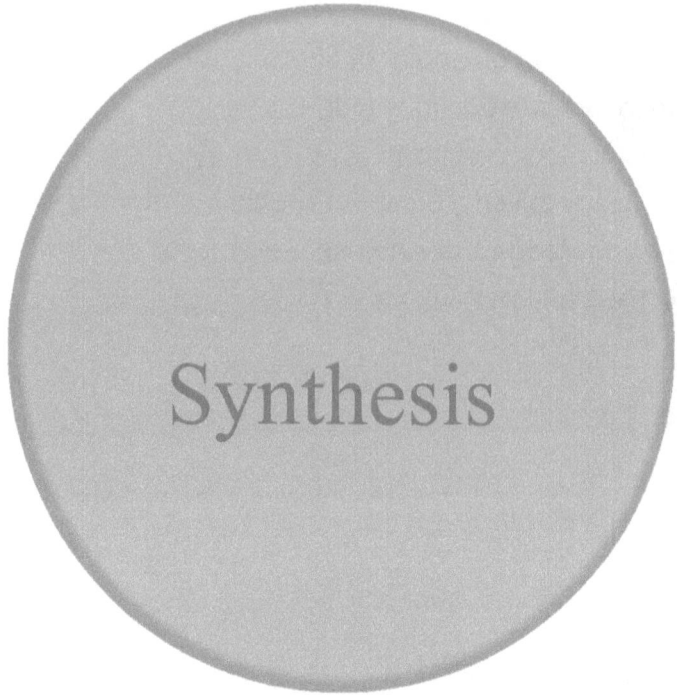

Synthesis

Synthesis is the third way we create new knowledge.

When charcoal is recovered from the refinery kiln, there is always a substantial collection of small bits and pieces of charcoal left over. This material is too small to sell. But charcoal manufacturers did not want to waste it either. By combining existing knowledge to form new knowledge, a solution was found. The existing knowledge was that charcoal is a natural fiber material just like wood. Its fiber creates surfaces so that, within a single gram of charcoal, there is a surface area estimated at 200 – 300 square meters. The other knowledge came from the paper industry, which had discovered that natural starches serve as a good binding agent for natural wood fibers. By mixing a starch and charcoal slurry and forming this mixture into balls and letting them dry out, one could create a lump of charcoal. This is how briquettes of charcoal are made. It allowed the manufacturers of charcoal to recover this waste and sell it as a product.[12]

What Edison was referring to when he spoke of "logical thinking" is synthesis. Synthesis occurs when we combine existing knowledge to create new knowledge. Synthesis includes analysis. Analysis is the act of discovering what existing knowledge we have about a particular object or problem. Synthesis combines this analytic knowledge with other knowledge we possess to form new knowledge.

One could argue that analysis by itself is a source of new knowledge. I would call it discovery, but in this case, it is not worth disagreeing over the point. You may be more comfortable thinking analysis creates new knowledge distinct from discovery. The point of the discussion is *innovation* and, for this purpose, I am including analysis as part of synthesis, because synthesis is where the solution to a problem is created.

The fact that we all synthesize and we do it often is perhaps the most interesting thing. For example, if you give this toy to a baby who has never seen it before, the baby will likely do a bit of discovery first.

---

12   The inventor of charcoal briquettes was none other than Henry Ford.

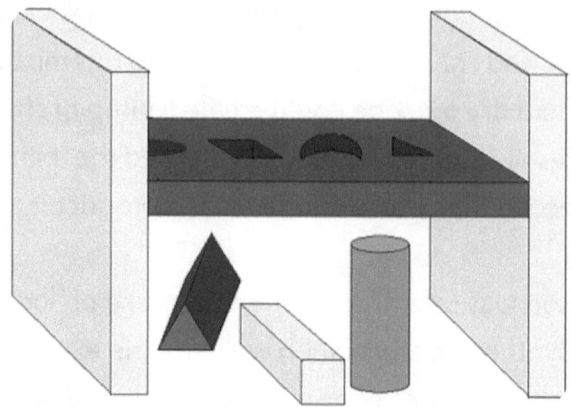

Shapes-and-holes cognitive learning toy

The child will pick up the blocks and look at the colors, discover the taste of each, test the hardness with some banging and throwing, etc. If you show the child that a block will fit in one of the holes, then the child will begin experimenting. The round block will be tried in the square hole, the triangle in the round hole, and so on, until, through a process of trial and error, the child will get all the blocks in the right holes. This is experimentation at work[13].

If you give the same toy to an adult, even one who has never seen the toy before, then the adult will be able to tell you which block goes in which hole without employing the trial-and-error approach the baby uses. The adult doesn't need to taste the blocks, be concerned with the colors, or know how far a block will travel when thrown. Nor is the adult going to need to try the square block in the round hole. Without consciously thinking about it, the adult's brain uses prior

---

13   Toddlers rarely solved the puzzle by putting the block at the hole and moving it around. Rather, they manipulated it in their hands before reaching the hole, they are doing a bit of analysis. See Helena Örnkloo and Claes von Hofsten, "Fitting objects into holes: On the development of spatial cognition skills," *Developmental Psychology* 43 vol. 2, (2007): 404-416.

knowledge about shapes to quickly realize the square-ended block goes in the square hole. The adult synthesizes the solution instantly.[14] When my father came up with water-filled balls to control air pockets when sinking a pipeline, he used synthesis. It is the most common method we use today to innovate solutions in business.

Combining Methods

We have three primary methods of innovation as I have described them: discovery, experimentation, and synthesis. While we've talked about them discreetly, it is usually the case that new knowledge is the result of combining two or all three toward the same solution. That is, we use some synthesis to set up efficient experiments, or we find some discovery in performing experiments as Fleming did. Just as the imaginary infant in the discussion of the blocks used discovery, experimentation, and finally synthesis to solve the problem, we often use all three tools to come to a workable result.

Synthesis has become the primary method today for developing new knowledge. Synthesis is the key skill for competing in the new normal of the twenty-first century. Historically, at first discovery may have played the most significant role, and later experimentation became more dominant. Today, synthesis has become the dominant method of creating new knowledge. Because synthesis depends on preexisting knowledge, and the Internet provides an efficient method of sharing information, we will continue to see synthesis dominate

---

14   New knowledge to the individual is not new knowledge to the human race. In innovation we seek new knowledge to the human race.

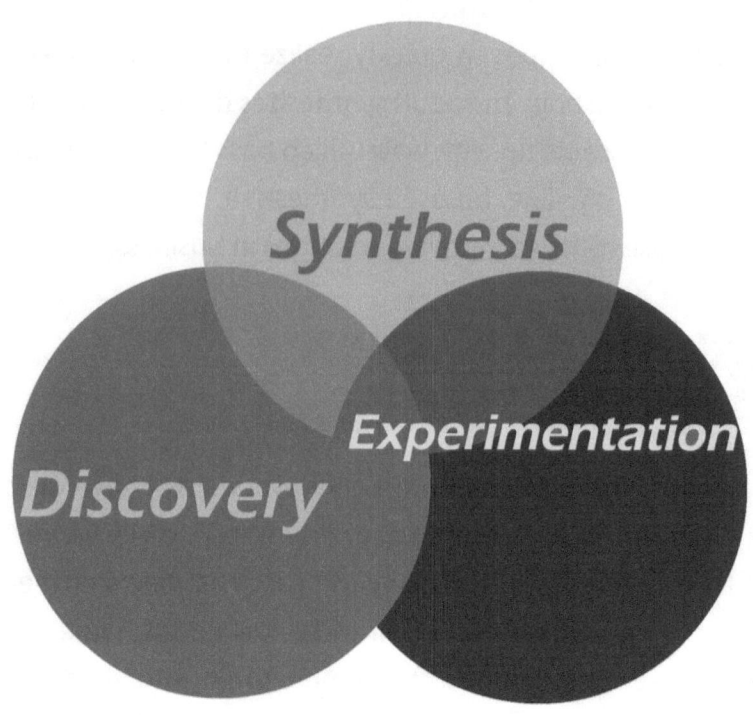

Often we combine all three methods in creating new knowledge.

the innovation landscape. However, knowledge isn't the only factor affecting the quantity or quality of synthesis. Thus, it is valuable to understand how it works and who is good at it, which we will explore in the next section.

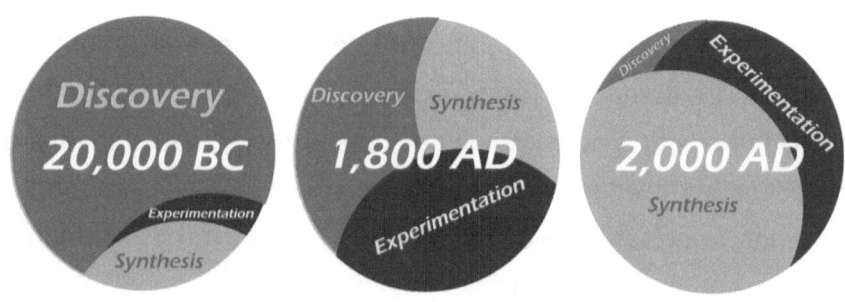

Historical Development of New Knowledge

Competitive advantage is how a company of people achieves and sustains success. It is based on unique knowledge. But, since the competition is also seeking advantage, it is a constant requirement that a company seeks new knowledge. Understanding what it takes to maximize a company's ability to create new knowledge is crucial to beating the competition at this game. We've laid out the three primary methods we use to create new knowledge and decided that synthesis is the crucial skill going forward. The leader in a company striving to be *the* competitive powerhouse understands it is important to get deep insight into talent of synthesis.

SYNTHESIS TALENT

When adults are faced with solving a problem, they fairly quickly make a choice on the most efficient approach. Some problems are tackled with a trial-and-error approach, while others are tackled with synthesis. We rarely tackle a problem by setting out on a directed discovery mission, e.g., looking for light bulb filament material in the Amazon forest as one of Edison's engineers did, or looking for water on the moon as NASA just accomplished.

If you have a problem for which it is believed that no knowledge exists that's applicable to solving the problem, then you are left with trial and error. For example, there are symmetric key encryption methods for which cryptographers believe there is no known way to discover the key, other than through brute force.[15] Brute force means trying every possible key until you find the right one. The security of a key is based on the key's length because the longer the key, the more tries are required to break it. To break a 128 bit key, you could need a few more than 340,282,366,920,938,463,463,374,607,431 billion tries. That's a lot of tries. If every second you could do 340,282,366,920,938, 463,463,374,607,431 tries, you'd need just over thirty-one years to try every possible key.

People interested in such things have worked on methods to build computers specifically designed to perform a lot of tries quickly. It is conceivable, of course, that someday a whiz kid will discover a mathematical flaw, something that was not previously realized, to

---

15 This assumes that the keys are housed securely, etc. The CIA maintains that it is easier to break into the computer that holds the plain-text document than to try to decrypt the document once it's been encrypted.

short-stop this trial-and-error process. But for now, we are left with only a trial-and-error process.

In other cases, when first faced with a problem to solve, it is not always immediately apparent that we already have the knowledge needed to synthesize a solution. In those cases, the most efficient approach is to start with trial and error and watch for opportunities to apply knowledge, which will allow us to shortcut the solution.

For example, if you want to devise a strategy to ensure you never lose at tic-tac-toe (naughts and crosses) whether you go first (the player using Xs) or second (using Os), then you are likely to pull out a sheet of paper and start putting Xs and Os in the three-by-three tic-tac-toe board. Fairly quickly, you will come up with a foolproof strategy. This approach starts with trial and error. If the game were played like football, right to the end, irrespective of the impossibility of the other team winning, there would be 362,000+ possible games. But the game ends when one player gets three in a row. This leaves just over 255,000 games. However, you do not need to go through the more than 255,000 possible games to develop a foolproof strategy.

That is because the trial-and-error approach either creates knowledge or knowledge becomes apparent, and you use that knowledge to synthesize shortcuts. For instance, if you are playing Xs, you move first. Suppose you decide your first move is to place your X mark in one of the middle-border squares (those marked with an A), you may realize that the game board is symmetrical. It makes no difference which A square you start with; the game that follows will be the same. That is, there aren't four different games because there are four A squares;

each A square is equivalent to the other three at the beginning of the game. The same is true if you started in the corner (B). You really only have three choices for your first move: any A, any B, or C not nine. Now you've cut the number of possible games by two-thirds and only have 85,000 possible games left.

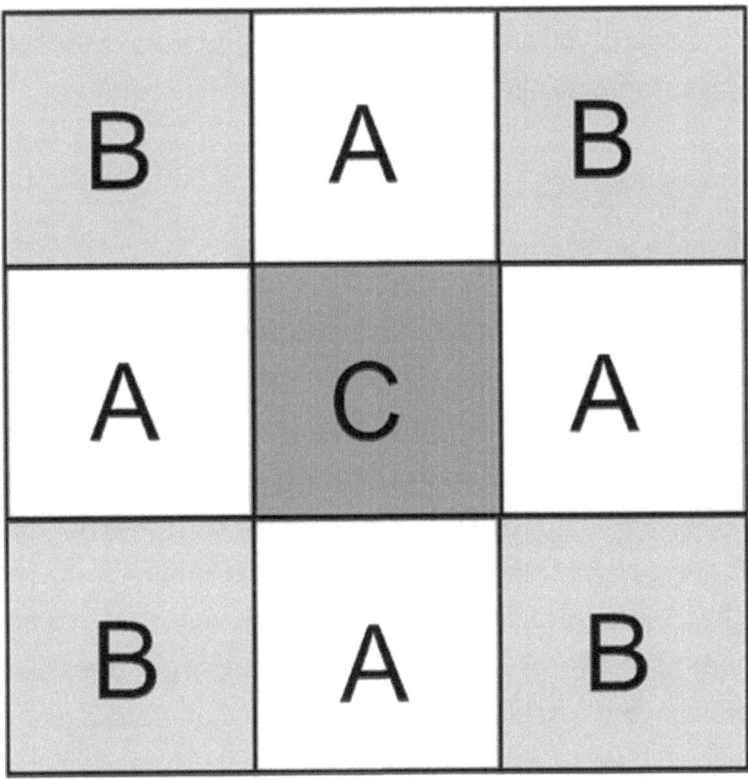

You are not going to go through all those possible games to come up with a strategy. That's because your objective is to *never lose*. If you are the player who goes first, you can build a strategy around always starting in the same place every time, say the very center square (C). You've reduced the possible games by two-thirds again, to 28,000. That leaves the opponent with eight squares to choose from. Since the grid is symmetrical, every A square is the same as every other A, and likewise, every B square is identical to every other B square. Thus, the opponent has two possible moves, not eight. That further reduces the play to 7,000 games.

Without going through the complete strategy development, you can see that using knowledge about possible moves and the geometry of the board, you are able to synthesize shortcuts to the solution. We do this automatically in our brains.

C.R.A.P.

Our brains have the automatic ability to see some solutions with a mental snap. It is the moment of insight that magically seems to pop into our brains. If you are a native English speaker, you may experience that snap with the following. (Apologies to those of you who are less familiar with English.) Compound remote associate problems, or C.R.A.P., are used for fascinating brain research by Mark Jung-Beeman at Northwestern University. He and Edward Bowden have compiled a list of these puzzles based on how quickly people get them. The puzzles involve word association. For example, what word is associated with each of these three words: man/stop/wrist? The answer is *watch*, as in watchman, stopwatch, and wristwatch. Try these four, each with a different answer:

cottage/swiss/cake
rocking/wheel/high
cream/skate/water
show/life/row

Chances are, with at least one of these, you experienced a brain snap, where the answer (cheese, chair, ice, boat) just popped into your head. It's a little weird because it's as if your brain does something that you really don't control or understand. That is why we say our mind seems to automatically find the solution. Neuroscientists like Beeman have done very interesting work in trying to understand what is taking place in the brain when we have these brain snaps, or when we take a bit longer to solve a puzzle. You may find with the following puzzles that you feel more like you are in control of the process. Most of us don't get these easily if at all. If you get even one, you're doing better than I did.

reading/service/stick
shadow/chart/drop
land/hand/house
cast/side/jump

Here you may have found yourself doing a great deal more search-ing, going through the catalogue in you mental dictionary of all the words that are associated with each of the words in the four puzzles. You are trying to force the synthesis through this knowledge review. The answers are lip, eye, farm, and broad.

Trial and Error or Synthesis?

There are other problems for which we have the knowledge to syn-thesize the answer, but trial and error appears to be a more efficient process. For example, consider the following sum-to-fifteen popular puzzle:

You must place each of the numbers one to nine in a three-by-three grid using all nine numbers so that the three numbers in any straight line, add (horizontally, vertically, or diagonally) to fifteen.

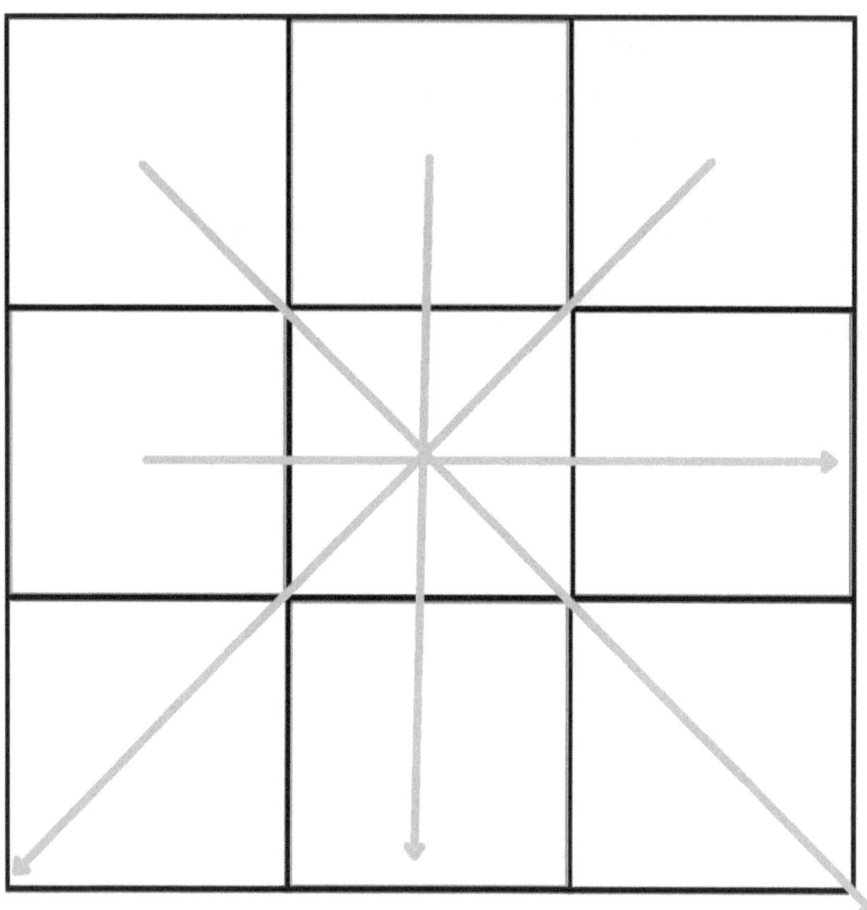

Sum 1-9 to exactly 15 diagonally, vertically and horizontally.

Almost all of us would tackle this problem using the trial-and-error method. That is because it is not immediately obvious that the synthesis approach would work, and trial and error will work. You could have chosen to solve this puzzle without using trial and error. Synthesis, in this case, is more challenging than trial and error. Synthesis requires that you are able to explain, with sound logic, why each number is placed where it is placed. If you like a challenge, this is a good one.

Synthesis, the only option.

Still other problems do not lend themselves to a trial-and-error approach. For these, we must use our ability to synthesize. The following simple puzzle is easier to solve using synthesis, mostly because few of us have two sandglasses that would allow us to perform trial and error. Even if you have a three-minute timer, you're unlikely to have a seven-minute timer. Moreover, the construct of the puzzle suggests that we really only get one try; otherwise, the eight minutes are gone.

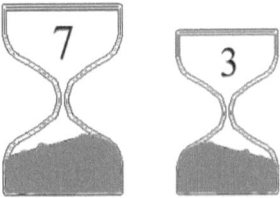

You need to measure eight minutes. You have two sand timers, one for seven minutes, and the other for three minutes.

How can you measure eight minutes using these two sand timers?

Solving this puzzle uses simple mathematics. Mathematical thinking is almost always synthesis even though it's almost never innovative.

So, why is synthesis important and useful to solve business problems? First, it is often the only way to approach a problem. It is hard to imagine how Tapline could have developed experiments in underwater pipeline installation to *find* the balls solution without having the idea first. Second, even when there are alternatives, synthesis is almost always a cheaper approach. Companies that rely heavily on trial-and-error solutions, such as a pharmaceutical company searching for a new drug, are constantly looking for ways to shortcut the number of trials they need to perform or for ways to run the trials faster and cheaper. In the case of drug researchers, if they had better knowledge of chemical properties and interactions with illnesses and the human body, they could use more mental synthesis and less experimentation to find effective drugs.

In the case at the back of the book, as the supervisor of the front/backend, Bobby Brinkman floated the idea of assigning an individual chargeback reason to each clerk. Sarah shot down this idea because the incoming volume for each reason code varied greatly and was unpredictable. She indicated that, at any time, some people would be inundated with cases, while others would have nothing to do. She insisted that was not an acceptable situation given that they were already severely backlogged.

Bobby used synthesis to come up with the solutions to work though the backlog and eliminate the $8 million loss rate. He saw the big picture and how all the details needed to fit together. It was then just a matter of solving the myriad small problems that made up the whole.

He used synthesis to come up with the solution that sidestepped Sarah's objection. In the end, he assigned individual reason codes to individual clerks because he wanted to ensure that every chargeback dispute had an owner. The owner had clear responsibility to work the case within the time frame. To deal with the ebbs and flows of volume, he allowed the workers to help each other and still get credit for the work done. By doubling up the productivity, Bobby ensured the chargebacks stayed current.

Clearly he did not use discovery or experimentation to come to this solution. Since he invented the way productivity allowed clerks to change desks, he could not have discovered the solution. Nor did he use experimentation. He simply thought it through clearly and used a combination of how people work, the fluctuation in incoming volumes, and that people will game any system to come up with a solution that works for the business and for the people working the chargeback desk.

Analytics and Serendipity

It is useful to understand that we have at least two types of synthesis that apply to problem solving. One is an analytic approach to problem solving, which is really the type of synthesis applicable to the puzzles above. With the analytic approach, the synthesizer sees patterns in the problem and reconfigures them logically to derive a solution. The element of synthesis in this process is the ability to pick out the relevant patterns that lead to the analytic solution. For example, in the sand -timer puzzle, a good synthesizer probably did not even consider that the imaginary timers were made of glass, that the glass is transparent, that the imaginary sand grains are of a certain size, that when they fall to the bottom they might form a cone initially, that if you took the timers to the moon, they would have to be recalibrated to different timers, and therefore the puzzle may be unsolvable, etc. These ideas are not relevant in coming to a logical solution.

Nobel Prize-winning physicist Richard Feynman was extraordinarily good at figuring out what knowledge was useful to solve a problem. In the book *Surely You're Joking Mr. Feynman*, he tells a story about how *lucky* he was one day when his friends at Princeton challenged him to solve for *e* to some power. He had started the challenge by saying it was easy to do, you just had to sum a series. It was a big series, not really something Feynman could do in his head really fast. But his friends asked him what's *e* to the 3.3? Almost instantly he replied 27.11.

Feynman wants to stop; he feels incredibly lucky that they gave him one he could do quickly because he broke it into mathematical parts that he already knew.[16] They then said e to the 3? Feynman couldn't believe his luck, "Twenty point zero eight five," he says. He tells them that's enough for one day, but one of them says e to the 1.4? "It's four point zero five," says Feynman. In his book, he explains how he solved each of these using different tricks. None of them were solved in the same way. He didn't know the answers in advance. That is, he hadn't memorized that e to the 3 is 20.085. He figured it out by employing some mathematical characteristics he knew well. He refused to do any more because he was certain he had just been extremely lucky with their choices.

Feynman wasn't really as lucky as the thought. He had an uncanny mental ability to see patterns in problems that made them simpler to solve. His brain could make great fast leaps that let him discover these shortcuts. Even so, he was using the analytic approach to solving the problem. He looked for some property of the problem that would lead to a solution.

The other kind of synthesis is what Frans Johansson calls "flash in the sky serendipity." It is similar to that moment of inspiration we talked about with the compound remote associate problems but different in one key way. In the C.R.A.P. (compound remote associate problems) examples, the solution is always obviously connected to the problem words, since they are all compound words.

---

16 From repeated calculations in physics, he knew the logarithm of 10 to the base e was 2.3026; thus he knew e to the power of 2.3026 is 10. Of course he also knew e to the power of 1 is 2.718283. Thus, e to the power of 3.3 was e to the power of 2.3 times e to the power of one or 10 times 2.718...or 27.18, which was a little high because of the .0026, and he corrected for it; thus his answer 27.11

In flash-in-the-sky serendipity, the knowledge used to solve the problem is not a property of the problem or in some other way obviously[17] connected. It is often expressed as a metaphor from some distant field. The memory pattern formed in acquiring the knowledge of the ping-pong-ball burp gun possibly coming to mind and matching up with the mental patterns represented in the problem of sinking a pipeline is an example of this. Often, however, the source of inspiration is less traceable, and the innovator is at a loss to describe where the idea came from.

Jung-Beeman is also working with John Kounios, a neuroscientist at Drexel University, to monitor what goes on in the brain when we have these moments of insight. Those of you who follow the notions of what the right and left brain does will not be surprised that there is a correlation between the moment of insight and a spike in activity in the right hemisphere. The researchers believe cells in the right side of the brain are active within a broader landscape than cells on the left side. They make more distant and unprecedented connections. The connections are unprecedented at least on a conscious level.

Work with rats at MIT's Picower Institute provides intriguing insight into how patterns are formed in the brain during learning. Researchers there have been looking directly at the memory-forming

---

17   Perhaps a better word here is *consciously* connected since the brain obviously made the connection; we are just not conscious of what the connection was. Research into how the brain creates memories has suggested that the brain evaluates experiences and categorizes them into known or new patterns. This allows the brain to be more economical in its processing. It is these memory patterns that allow the brain to make these great metaphorical leaps to create new solutions.

mechanics by studying living rats using technology that allows them to monitor the synaptic activity in the rats' brains. Sleep plays a key role in how rats construct and retain success patterns. In a maze, the rats run and then stop for a few moments, run and stop, run and stop, etc. When they stop, their brains fire the same sequence of hippocampal cells that fired when they were running, except very rapidly and in reverse order. Also, the sequence represents the entire track not just the sequence of patterns between stops.

Later, when the rat is asleep, during slow-wave sleep, the sequence is again observed as played back very rapidly, in proper order, but skipping the stop points. Finally, in REM sleep, the patterns appear again, in proper sequence and in near real time. The brain is using replay while awake and replay while asleep to organize the synaptic patterns to create a memory pattern.

Experiential evidence also suggests that human brains function similarly during stop and sleep periods. People often find they do their best problem solving while doing things like showering (a mental stop cycle). Some people report waking up from a nap having solved a problem apparently while asleep. It makes sense that our brains are working on pattern processing during those periods, just as rats do.

However, it is possible that much more is going on. That is, the connections that Jung-Beeman sees as unprecedented may turn out to be sort of prerecorded. It is possible that in the background, as knowledge is acquired, it is broken apart into its characteristics that will later allow the brain to search across the knowledge bank for that kind of characteristic. For example, in the case of the ping-pong-ball burp gun, when my father processed his analysis of the burp gun, his brain may have stored things like:

> *A ball that is almost the size of the diameter of a tube will act as a one-way valve as a fluid substance is pressed against one side of the ball when it is in the tube. Leakage can only go one way. Also, the ball can be propelled along when the pressure on one side of the ball is sufficiently greater than the pressure on the other side of the ball.*

Thus, when my father looked at the pipeline process, his brain went looking for a way to stop one fluid substance (air) from leaking into another fluid substance (water). His brain may have had many references to leakage, but when the concept of pipe (tube) was added, the brain could offer up the ball-in-the-tube memory. This is all speculation. We do not yet know how this works in the brain; it just does.

How we process incoming information is an indicator of our problem-solving abilities. Good synthesizers can take incoming information, knead it, turn it around, look at it from top to bottom, and absorb something fundamental, as they process it into knowledge.

People who are strong synthesizers certainly can easily solve puzzles such as the examples here. The single most valuable skill in finding solutions is the ability to completely and correctly define or redefine the problem. This is a skill useful in both synthesizing through the logical analysis method and synthesis that's flash in the sky serendipity. These may just be the same thing. Kounios and Jung-Beeman suggest more is happening in the brain when we have these flashes of inspiration. It may be that it is not so much a *flash* as a process. The process may be the same, whether or not we are conscious of it during analysis, when we wake from a nap with a brilliant solution, or when the word *bill* pops into our brains when we look at duck/fold/dollar.

Supersynthesizers have the ability and inclination to see the problem from different angles. As a young physicist, Feynman was nominated to the Manhattan project because of his legendary problem-solving/synthesis ability. Oppenheimer did not use the word synthesis, he just knew from stories in the physics community that Feynman had a great mind for problem solving. True to his reputation, Feynman proved his problem-solving skill right from the start. He was first sent to the University of Chicago, where Enrico Fermi led the team building the first nuclear reactor. The scientists there had heard this whiz kid was coming, and on his first day, they presented him with a mathematical problem that had been vexing the team there for more than a month. He looked at it for a few moments and then showed them the solution. It was a great example of seeing the problem from a completely different angle. He showed them that it wasn't really one problem at all but two. When he laid out the two problems, all the mathematicians in the room could easily see the solution. Often precisely redefining the problem exposes the solution.

For example, take the puzzle below.

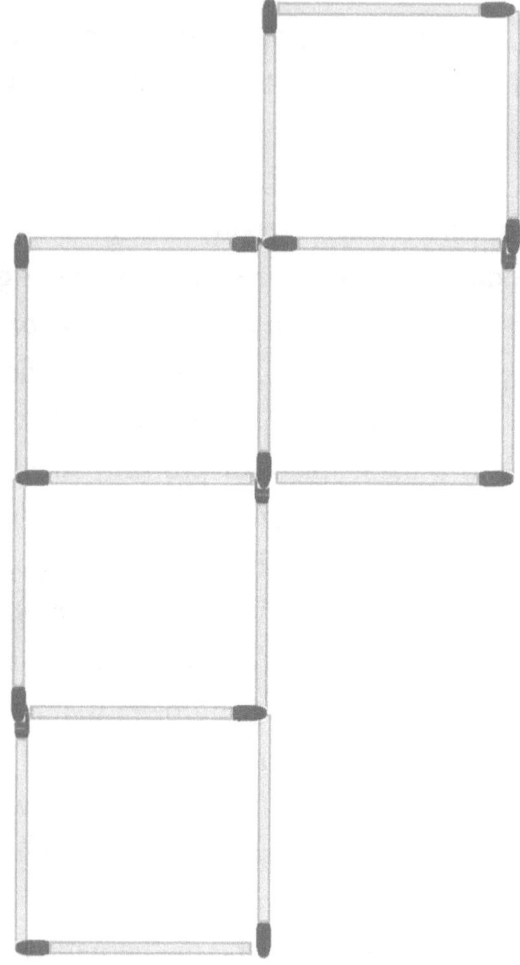

Matchstick puzzle.

Puzzle: This figure is made up of matchsticks laid out to form these five squares. Reposition two (and only two) matches to form four equal squares, each with the same size and shape as the individual original five squares. You may not overlap one match on top of the other.

Most of us would tackle this by first looking for a solution rather than looking for an opportunity to redefine the problem. We would look for a match or two matches that we could remove and eliminate a box. Then, we'd figure out where to use those matches so that we ended up with four boxes. We might do a lot of mental trial and error and with enough persistence, either solve the puzzle or go crazy. If you are interested in doing this on your own, stop reading here and come back when you're crazy.

A supersynthesizer is a person with unusually strong problem-solving talents. The supersynthesizer sees patterns in problems differently from the rest of us. Instead of looking for a solution, a supersynthesizer might look at the problem and see if there is a different point of view. Instead of thinking, "I'll start by picking up two matches," the supersynthesizer might think, "I have to place two matches here so that they will each be a side to a box. I cannot place these two matches where a match exists already because I would either be overlaying a match or just putting a match back where it was. Thus, I need to find a new spot where I can place two matches and form a box that is not already formed."

This divides the problem into two separate steps, and in reverse order of the way most of us would attempt a solution. By taking this approach, the supersynthesizer quickly sees that there are only two places where a new box can be formed with two matches: at the top just to the left of the top box (marked A) and to the right of the second box just below the first box in the right column (marked F).

Or the supersynthesizer might think, "I have sixteen matches, and I need to make four boxes." (How many of us would have even thought to count the matches?) "Each box has four sides, four times four equals sixteen, therefore, no squares can share a match on a side because then I'd only be using fifteen matches. If they touch at all, they can only touch at corners. This means that you cannot use the two matches to form a box at A. Square A currently shares a side with both C and B. Since it can only touch on a corner, that would mean it touches square D because C and B each share a match with A, so we would need to eliminate both C and B. While you could eliminate box C by just removing one match (the left vertical match in C leaving boxes A, D, and E), you cannot do the same with box B. To eliminate B, you would need to remove both the top-most match and the right vertical match. Eliminating both C and B would require moving three matches. Since you can only move two matches, you cannot remove both C and B. That means A cannot be where we create a new box. Thus, the new square has to be at F."

Alternately the synthesizer might say, "Since I cannot form a square at H with only two matches, I cannot take one or two matches from the bottom box (G) without leaving a match just hanging out. The same is true of the top box (B), if you use two matches from B to form the new box at F. Therefore, boxes B and G must remain. And thinking that through, if the only place the boxes can touch is at the corners, and I already know that I must have boxes B, G, and F, then I must be left with boxes at B, C, F, and G. Therefore, I must eliminate boxes D and E. In each case, I need three of their matches for other boxes, thus I must take the unused match, the outer match in boxes D and E, which eliminates the boxes and gives me the matches to form F.

By looking at the problem from a different perspective, we analyze and synthesize it differently. This makes the solution easier to reach, if you didn't get a flash of insight that solved the problem for you or you couldn't get it by trial and error.

In a business context, the obvious solution often isn't apparent until someone comes along and redefines the problem. Of course, we can easily imagine that a suggestion like, "Let's don't think about moving two matches; rather, let's start by adding two matches," would get a response like, "Look, we're trying to solve a problem here that is exactly about moving two matches. Just stay out of the way if you don't have something useful to add."

Synthesis is a human talent, and like most talents, some people are better at it than others. In the case of synthesis, perhaps it is an innate talent or one that can be improved with practice. Perhaps, like playing a musical instrument, it's some mix of the two.

I have been asked if someone can be taught to be a great synthesizer. In general, the crucial element in becoming extraordinarily good at anything is either some natural gift or a deep, enduring passion that drives hours and hours of practice. Thus, perhaps you could study the techniques used to analyze and synthesize, but without a great passion for problem solving, you may not reach that level of superior talent. Perhaps a good litmus test is whether you stopped reading at the mention of the matchstick puzzle, so that you could solve it. Did you find a way to solve the sum to fifteen puzzle using synthesis, rather than trial and error, or are you saving the puzzle for that perfect moment when you can dedicate yourself to its challenge? If your answer is yes, then you probably have the passion.

The other ingredient that makes for a great synthesizer is broad knowledge. The patterns that pop into our brains as solutions to problems are patterns created as our brains store knowledge and experience. The more breadth to the patterns, the more likely our brains will find a matching pattern. Synthesizers like Feynman draw from broad knowledge. In the case of Feynman, it is said that had he been interested in publishing his work in other fields of study, he could easily have won an additional Nobel Prize or two. He had deep curiosity about many things he pursued, and this knowledge provided the framework of patterns that his mind used so fruitfully. For this reason (and another reason that I will talk about later), a company will always benefit from everyone in the company pursuing learning as an ongoing activity.

PROBLEMS IN PROBLEM SOLVING

The biggest challenge in problem solving is getting the problem right—not finding the solution. Sometimes, we just approach the problem backward, and we end up squeezing the problem into the solution.

Smart Cards

This is what is happening in the credit card industry with the counterfeit fraud problem. The obvious technical answer was to use the security available from a smart card. Since the beginning of the 1990s, smart card manufacturers have been working with the credit card industry to find a business case that supports the product. The credit card industry loses hundreds of millions of dollars every year from this one kind of fraud. But the implementation of smart cards costs billions. The cost of the solution exceeds the cost of the problem by a huge margin. To cover that cost, lots of nonfraud-related applications have been suggested over the years, but all have failed to generate revenues that might fill the gap.

This has not stopped countries like the UK and France from implementing smart cards and squeezing the problem into the solution.

Points of View

Another type of problem is being so close to your product you don't even think to ask the one important question—will it resonate with customers? When Google entered the South Korea and China markets, no one thought to ask, "Is our minimalist screen approach going to resonate in these countries?" Of course, if it had, it wouldn't be an example here. It turns out that the Chinese and Koreans like a much busier and more entertaining screen. Google's simple screen did not meet their new customers' expectations.[18]

The most common type of difficulty we see when we define a problem poorly is to assume that we already fully understand the issues. Typically, we gather a bunch of our internal company experts in the room and define the problem. This is an insidious trap. We cannot tell we are in this trap, and we often are. This chapter discusses what it is, why it happens, and how to overcome it.

Facts aren't facts unless we *let* them be facts.

A JOKE:

> *A fellow walks into a crowded bar and orders three beers. He drinks them by taking a sip from the first beer, then a sip from the second, then a sip from the third, and then back to the first, and so on. When he's finished, he orders a second round of three beers. The bartender, being helpful,*

---

18   Global instincts, local flavours on the Web. The Hindu, Accessed :11/19/2009 URL: http://www.thehindu.com/2008/07/30/stories/2008073061692200.htm
Google's New 'Animated' Home Page In Korea, by Greg Sterling, Accessed 11/19/2009 URL: http://searchengineland.com/googles-new-animated-home-page-in-korea-11329

suggests, "You know, if you order the beers one at a time, they won't go flat before you get to the bottom."

"Oh, I know," says the fellow. "But I do this for my brothers. You see Samuel is off in Asia, and Michael is in South America. We agreed that every day we would drink a beer for each other, so the three of us would keep each other in our thoughts, and I'm having two rounds today because I missed yesterday."

"What a lovely ritual!" says the bartender.

Well, the fellow becomes a regular in the bar, drinking his three beers this way every day. One day he comes in and sits at the bar and orders just two beers. The bar goes quiet with concerned looks passing across the patrons' faces. The bartender gently places the two beers in front of the fellow who immediately begins his sipping ritual. The bartender leans forward and in a soft voice says, "I am very sorry, and I want to express my condolences..."

"Oh, no!" says the fellow looking up. "No. Everyone is fine. Both my brothers are well. It's me, you see. I've become a Mormon and have given up drinking."

The joke about the fellow drinking the three beers is funny because we assume his action of drinking the two beers is inconsistent with his values. In their book *Tuned In*, Craig Stull, Phil Myers, and David Meerman Scott suggest that whenever someone is arguing some point while trying to make a marketing or promotional decision and starts the sentence with "I think," then the proper response is "Your opinion, although interesting, is irrelevant." Their point is simple. Don't assume you see the world the way your potential customers do. If you're going to be successful in solving customers' problems, you need to see the problems from their perspective not your own.

The joke about our beer-drinking fellow isn't funny at all if we assume that he is a reasonably intelligent person, and his drinking the two beers *is* consistent with his overall view of the world. It is not a possibility we entertain. Is this possible? Of course it is. First, the story is fiction. In fiction, anything is possible. Think outside the box and imagine that, in his culture, actions that you take on behalf of someone else at their request are their actions not your own. Thus, it is his brothers who are drinking the two beers not our fellow. He bears the burden of feeling the effects of his brothers' drinking. But he, as himself, is abstaining, consistent with his personal values. This is a far-fetched fictional example, but often, getting a clear picture of a problem requires looking at it and recognizing what is a fact and what isn't. Sometimes the facts appears far-fetched to those who are supposed to be experts in the matter.

This is what happened to Google in Korea and China. If anyone had suggested to Google that the nearly blank Google screen wouldn't resonate in Korea and China, they would have gotten disbelieving looks. It's because it doesn't even occur to us that there could be a different perspective. Just as it would not have occurred to any of us that our beer-drinking friend could come from a very different cultural perspective. You must get the *problem* right or the solution will miss the mark.

Experts: Breathing Their Own Exhaust

When we rely on our internal experts, we fall into the trap almost right away. Experts are just as susceptible to missing the difference between what they think is true and what is true as anyone else. Often, the expert is more likely to miss the truth because he or she has locked in on something long believed to be true. Being an expert is sometimes an almost irrepressible handicap.

CASE EXAMPLE:

Sarah Macintosh worked in the chargeback department for several years. Her mindset about the work was formed as a result of years of exposure to the same process and point of view. It wasn't that she had some doubts about Bobby Brinkman's ideas. She had no doubt—his ideas were unworkable. They did not fit the problem. Of course she was mistaken.

Sarah's mindset concerning these issues led her to make decisions that were completely wrong. Many companies would have fired Sarah when it became apparent that she was a big part of the problem. She was fortunate that she worked for a paternal (versus a paternalistic) company.

*When she took a new assignment, her latent capabilities to lead an organization were unleashed. She came to her new role with no mindset. This freed her to listen to the people in her new area. It is almost always the case that internal, junior people have deep insight into the problems and how to fix them. A **new** manager can listen to these ideas without filtering everything though a very narrow mindset.*

Sarah was very successful in this new assignment.

mindset is a difficult thing to displace

Perhaps one of the most dramatic examples of *mindset* is what happened before Einstein came up with his theory of relativity. Newtonian physics says that if you are standing still and throw a ball with a certain force X, it will leave your hand at fifty kilometers per hour. Likewise, if you are standing on a train going sixty kilometers per hour, and you throw the ball with the same force X, it will leave your hand at one hundred ten kilometers per hour (fifty + sixty). In 1887, E.W. Morley and A.A. Michelson decided to measure the difference between the velocities of light as it is beamed with the speed of the rotation of the earth pushing it and as it is beamed perpendicular to the rotation of the earth. The idea was that the light beam that has the speed of the earth's rotation behind it must be going faster than the light beam that does not have that incremental speed behind it. To their surprise, no difference was detected. The scientific community *knew* there was something was wrong with the way they did their experiment because you cannot violate the laws of physics. It perplexed scientists for years because they couldn't find the error.

Is this so surprising? One possible explanation is that the earth is not rotating. "WHAT?" just went through your brain didn't it? The certainty we have about the earth rotating is the same certainty those scientists had about Newtonian physics. They could not have contemplated the alternative.

Recognizing facts is essential to getting the problem right, but point of view can color the evidence and cause us to interpret the evidence in a way that's consistent with our worldview. It is a phenomenon that has been noticed and written about repeatedly in business and psychology texts. It is often expressed as *being too close to the problem* and, thus, not able to see it clearly. Einstein said, "What does a fish know about the water it swims in?"

When Albert Einstein looked at the Michelson-Morely velocity of light results, he thought to himself, 'What if the results of the experiment are correct?' What Einstein did was step back from the problem. If the evidence proved correct, that would mean Newtonian physics was wrong. This heresy opened the universe to a new point of view and changed physics forever. Everything is relative.

Even relativity can get you into trouble:

> *A fellow was having a hell of a time driving down the highway. Suddenly, his phone rang, and when he picked it up, his wife said, "Hey, if you're on Route 8, watch out! The radio just reported there's a guy driving the wrong way on the highway!*
>
> *"Heck," shouted the fellow. "It's not just one car. It's all of them!"*

Did this fellow let his point of view color his interpretation of the facts? We have a natural bias to view things so that they are consistent with our view of the world or a particular position we've taken. We often filter information to be consistent with our beliefs.

Jeffery Pfeffer and Robert Sutton,[19] both professors at Stanford and authors of marvelous business books, wrote an article for the *Harvard Business Review* on evidence-based decision making. In it, they take to

---

19 Of Sutton's books I encourage anyone aspiring to be a great business leader to read *The No Asshole Rule and Weird Ideas That Work.* Both are insightful and fun to read.

task a number of management practices, like forced ranking and rank and yank, which involve moving people frequently and thus having little team continuity or time in position longevity. They make a point in this article about evidence, which on reflection is ironic.

They note that there is plenty of evidence to support the fact that *performance improves with team continuity and time in position.* They give great evidence to support the idea, for example, the successful U.S. women's soccer team whose core group played together for thirteen years and knew where the other players would be and what they would do on the field. This time in position and continuity is what made the team so successful. Other examples given were surgical teams, string quartets, cockpit crews, and top management. Interestingly, my brother-in-law is a commercial airline pilot, and I don't think he flies with the same people in the cockpit very often.

The examples (soccer teams, surgical teams, string quartets) intuitively support the notion that, in those circumstances, you'd expect performance to be better when the team had been together for a long time. In these examples, you're not expecting much in the way of change. You wouldn't expect someone in your string quartet to start playing Bach concertos in a completely new way. Or a heart surgery team to suddenly try something new while you're on the operating table for a routine procedure. Although, in the heart surgery example, the time in position of the surgeon may be more important than the continuity of team.

Certainly, for a precision flying team like the Blue Angels, it would be important to have history with your fellow pilots when you fly inverted, surrounded by five other planes, each only eighteen inches apart. Sutton's and Pfeffer's reference to top management is sometimes true but not always. As we will see, when you repeat something over and over again, you become very good at it. Unfortunately your brain narrows in on what it takes to do the repeated tasks, and ignores "irrelevant" information. When the problem itself mutates, often the clues that change is needed are hidden in this ignored information. Where you need to maintain competitive advantage through innovation, your brain can handicap you because it is working to keep you good at the old way, and it is failing to pay attention to the new clues. (See below for an example of how successful you can be retaining continuity of team while eliminating time in position.)

TIME IN POSITION = MINDSET

An Australian company had been losing market share, and now the business was no longer generating a profit. Moreover, the franchise owners realized a recession was beginning. Under pressure, the CEO ran the company like a tyrant, causing the staff to avoid interactions with him as much as possible. As a result, he was not getting information about problems from his staff. The owners were looking ahead to a bleak future and decided to get out. They managed a fire sale, turning the company over to a local airline.

The airline's board made only one change—they hired a new CEO named Grant Halverson. Grant had a huge challenge facing him—both an immediate business turnaround and an oncoming recession. Luckily, he had great insight. He took the view that conventional wisdom should be treasured as past experience, but it created mindset, and mindset should not rule the day. Past experience is useful in evaluating future action, but mindset discounts alternatives to the status quo. One of the inspired changes he made was to move around the senior-executive responsibilities. Each of his direct reports received a new functional responsibility and gave up his or her old responsibility. To succeed in this environment, each executive had to work closely with his or her predecessor.

Each brought a fresh perspective, unburdened by mindset, to his or her new role. New managers ask questions that no longer occur to old managers. Kerry Miles had been managing IT and was given the responsibility for operations, including fraud operations. Kerry brought a fresh mind to operations and fraud. She noted "My systems background helped. I knew what I could get out of IT to support changes in my new area of responsibility." Likewise, the executive with sales experience took over managing customer service and application processing. His years of face-to-face contact with the customer allowed him to bring that perspective to both functions and help the team see things from the customer's point of view. This was especially true for the application-processing people, because they hadn't thought of the applicant as an actual customer or a future customer. Each of the remaining executives was given a new role as well, and a new IT manager was hired.

This strategy delivered short-term and medium-term benefits, and de-livered spectacular long-term results for the company once the recession ended.

In the short term, new managers, who are unfamiliar with the work, walked into their roles without a mindset. With the mindset gone, work-ers throughout the company who'd been sitting on an idea (like the worker in the fabric factory) could bring the idea forward. In the short term, they could immediately implement a series of relatively small, safe changes that improved efficiency and effectiveness. These changes didn't alter the products and services provided; they just made them cheaper to deliver. These incremental improvements freed funds for fur-ther investment. Medium-term improvements comprised the next level of ideas. These changed and improved the products and services offered. Finally, the longer-term ideas created new products and services that allowed the business to expand its customer base.

The effects for the Australian business in the years following the reces-sion were phenomenal. Sales grew from A$400 million to A$ 6.4 billion, the number of customers grew from 145,000 to 450,000, while average customer spending grew sevenfold. During this period, ROE reached 35 *percent after taxes, and market share grew from 4 percent to 16 percent, which matched their best competitor.*

People who have been in place for a long time can be like the pre-Einstein physicists, and naturally see the situation from a highly biased perspective. In these circumstances, where change is needed, sometimes the *best* thing you can do *is* bring in new team members with a fresh perspective.

That's what Bill Ford had in mind in 2006, when he brought in a new CEO with no automobile experience. Alan Mulally is an engineer, and before taking the reins at Ford Motor Company, he'd built airplanes for Boeing. His fresh perspective and lack of mindset has enabled him to ask questions that executives within the industry would not think needed asking. He also got new answers that enabled Ford to position itself ahead of its domestic rivals. At the time of this writing Ford is the only U.S. auto company with much hope of surviving intact.

We will explore later why this *novice strategy* works well. The point of this discussion is to always strive to get the facts and use unbiased logic to draw conclusions. It is easy to get trapped, especially when we use what we think is true as evidence without verifying it.

What tripped up Pfeffer and Sutton was that they took valid evidence for a particular situation (performance improves with continuity of team and time in position) and generalized it across all situations. Sometimes that is true, and sometimes it's clearly not.

Sometime the point of view is so rigid that the person will be incapable of seeing the issue from a different perspective.

Another joke:

A man showed up at a psychiatrist's office worried.

"Doc," he said. "I am worried about my family."

"Why is that? asked the doctor.

"Well, it seems they are having a hard time accepting the tragedy of my death," the man replied.

"Oh, I am sorry," responded the doctor. "Are you terminally ill?"

The man frowned at the psychiatrist. "Why? Do I look sick? No, I'm not sick. I'm dead!"

Surprised, the psychiatrist said, "Did you say you're dead?"

"Yes," replied the man. "Quite and completely dead!"

Intrigued, the psychiatrist invited the man to sit on his couch.

"So, you're dead, you say," inquired the doctor. "How long have you been dead?"

"Well," replied the man. "I've been dead most of my life, so to speak, since I am not really alive."

"Let me ask you something," said the psychiatrist, thinking. "Do dead people breathe?"

"No, don't be stupid. Of course dead people don't breathe," replied the dead man.

"Well, I have news for you," said the doctor triumphantly. "Clearly you're breathing, so you cannot truly be dead!"

"Oh, No! No!" laughed the man. "I am only pretending to breathe. It's a habit because not breathing tends to alarm people around me."

"Ah, I see," the doctor scratched his chin thoughtfully. "Well, do dead people's hearts beat?"

"Come on," answered the patient. "You know the answer to that. Of course dead people's hearts don't beat."

The psychiatrist walked over to his desk and pulled a stethoscope from a drawer, put the earpieces into his ears, and listened to the man's chest. "I hear a heartbeat," he said, raising his eyebrows to the dead man.

"Oh, that is just a sound I make. It's a habit like breathing," replied the man.

The doctor retuned to his desk, put the stethoscope away, and surreptitiously picked up a pin.

"So, if your heart is not beating then you would have no blood pressure, and you would not bleed?" he asked the patient.

"No! Of course not, dead people don't bleed," he said emphatically.

"Are you sure?" asked the doctor.

"Absolutely."

"If you got a cut, would you bleed?

"Look," replied the man impatiently. "Don't be thick about this. You know perfectly well I would not!"

Instantly, the doctor grabbed the man's finger and pricked it with the pin. Blood oozed out of the hole.

"Ah, ha!" exclaimed the doctor. "You see, you do bleed. You're alive!"

The man looked at his finger in bewilderment and then looked at the doctor with astonishment.

"Well, what do you know," he said throwing his hands up. "Dead people do bleed!"

A point of view can create a powerful bias.

Creating Mindset

Neuroscience researchers at MIT's Picower Institute, UC Berkeley, and UC San Francisco, and others, are helping to explain cognitive brain function. This fascinating research examines learning and formation of memory patterns. The most interesting research is being done at MIT monitoring synaptic electrical and chemical activity in the brains of rats. I don't know if rats can synthesize at all, but I am reasonably sure they don't do what humans do in combining unrelated knowledge to solve problems. Thus, the research on rats may only point in the right direction here.

The research does say that with lots of repetition, rats remember what they learn. After fifty or so repetitions, the rats will remember the maze for a year. With about 200 repetitions, the rat will hold the memory for life. The brain's ability to select and then retain *successful* behavior patterns is probably a key to survival. The evidence that a rat remembers a maze is the way it runs straight though the maze without exploring alternatives. In the case of humans, we appear to be natural experimenters. If we didn't have this capability to identify and repeat successful patterns, we'd end up always trying something different. Ask anyone who runs experiments and they will tell you to expect many times more failures than successes. If we constantly experimented with new behaviors, we would fail a lot. Failing most all the time would not be a good path to survival.

The most interesting phenomenon is that once a success pattern is imprinted, repetition makes it more rigid. New data coming in is manipulated to the extent possible to fit with the existing pattern. Einstein knew this firsthand. His original work happened because he thought it through before he knew the rules—that is, before he was encumbered with a rigid pattern. He said, "The only thing that interferes with my learning is my education." He knew his ability to see something new depended on not embracing what was already there.

When he was older and had developed his own theories, he recognized the limitations he created for himself in his own brain. "It is the **theory** that decides what *can* be observed." He didn't say "what *may* be observed." He understood the affect on the brain of a deep-seeded pattern. Our pattern-development process makes it difficult for us to recognize any change to a previously successful pattern as a good change.

New good ideas mean change. Change is an affront to established success patterns in the brain. The initial negative response to a new idea may not seem that rational in hindsight, but in that immediate instant the response is seen as rational and correct. It is not as if you *think* the idea *may* not be so good. It's that you *know* the idea *is* bad since it opposes the success pattern. You can imagine how ridiculous our dead fellow in the story about the psychiatrist will feel when he suddenly realizes that he really isn't dead. In business, this failure to overcome your predisposition toward the facts can lead you into trouble. Christopher Morley wrote, "There is no squabbling so violent as that between people who accepted an idea yesterday and those who will accept the same idea tomorrow."

One of the most tangible ways to understand this phenomenon is to look at how we view music. Most of us have songs we love. We've listened to these songs many times. The more we listen to them, the more we like them (up to a point). The brain has created a pleasure pattern around these familiar sound patterns. Likewise, many of us have heard sounds from other cultures that they call *music* and we call *noise*. In his wonderful little book *Proust Was a Neuroscientist*, Jonah Lehrer talks about the brain's elasticity and our response to unfamiliar music. He describes the night in 1913, when Igor Stravinsky premiered his *Rite of Spring* in Paris. The orchestra first played Chopin. Then, without an intermission went straight into the dissonant sounds of the *Rite*. No ears in the audience were prepared for the sounds coming from the orchestra. The human brain manages to filter most of the elements of the sound created by instruments to focus on the common pitch across multiple instruments, even though the other qualities of the sounds are quite distinct. Music actually overwhelms the brain's ability to process information; it cannot decode all the sound information coming in, so it zooms in on the pitch and builds patterns around the changes in pitch, ignoring the other sound information. Our sense of music is the changes in pitch across a short period of time. The vividness of a sound is short lived. Our brain builds an anticipation of the upcoming pitch, even in unfamiliar music. It is either gratified in its anticipation or pleasantly surprised. But, if the change is radically different from what is expected, then the brain struggles with the pattern. Stravinsky composed the *Rite* to do just that.

The music so upset the crowd that they rioted and nearly destroyed the theatre.[20] This brought immediate notoriety to the music, and everyone wanted to hear this piece. It was then played for many audiences. Over time, people's brains got used to the sounds and were able to anticipate the changes in pitch because these changes had become familiar. It gained acceptance as music, and you've probably heard this music—Walt Disney included it in the classic *Fantasia*.

---

20   The riot may not have been only about the music. The ballet, too, was very different from what the crowd was used to. Also, there were sexual overtones in the dancing as well as political and social issues around the opening.

The elasticity of the patterns in our brains depends on how strongly we hold the concepts they represent. Religion and politics are topics we avoid when we first meet new people. That's because most of us have strongly held beliefs around both. In preparing for this work, we conducted an online survey of people's inclination to influence or be influenced when arguments for the opposing positions are presented. Here is how we set it up (This was done just at the end of President Bush's term in office):

> Many people in America have a strong opinion with regard to our president. Some people think Mr. Bush is a great president. Some people think Mr. Bush is an awful president. (We are not asking for your personal political views.)

We asked just three questions:

1. I have a strongly held opinion on this matter.
   ☐ True   ☐ False
2. Imagine you are given a day or two to prepare your arguments, and now you are given the opportunity to spend an uninterrupted thirty minutes to lay out your arguments supporting why you are right in holding your view of Mr. Bush. Suppose the person listening to you is just as intelligent as you but has a view that is directly opposite of your own. What is the probability that you will be persuasive enough to change that person's mind? Indicate that probability using a scale of 0 to 10, 0 being that you are certain you will *not* change that person's mind and 10

being that you are certain you will change that person's mind.

☐ 0 ☐ >0 and <1 ☐ 1-2 ☐ 2-3 ☐ 3-4 ☐ 4-7 ☐ >7 and < 10 ☐ 10

3. Imagine you are listening to someone who is just as intelligent as you, and who has a view of Mr. Bush that is directly opposite your own. You let this person speak uninterrupted for thirty minutes, putting forth his arguments for why his view is correct. What is the probability that you will be persuaded to change your mind after the thirty minutes?

☐ 0 ☐ >0 and <1 ☐ 1-2 ☐ 2-3 ☐ 3-4 ☐ 4-7 ☐ >7 and < 10 ☐ 10

People who said they did not have a strongly held position made up less than 20 percent of the responses. They felt that their ability to change someone else's mind was between 4 and 5 on our scale. Likewise, though just slightly lower, they felt someone else could influence them at between 4 and 5 on our scale.

However, people who indicated they held strong positions on the question felt the probability they could influence someone else at almost exactly 3 on the scale. But when it came to someone else being able to influence them, they felt it was much less likely, at 1.7 on our scale.

The key point of the survey was to underline that strongly held positions are not very susceptible to influence. People who see GWB as a great president interpret new events to be consistent with that model. While people who see GWB as an awful president interpret the same events consistent with their model. Exactly the same events reinforce these two opposite points of view.

Take the firing of the U.S. Attorneys. One side argues that U.S. Attorneys serve at the president's pleasure, and he can fire them at will. They point out that Bill Clinton, a democrat, did exactly the same thing when he came into office. Any discussion of differences in the circumstances is just splitting hairs. Behind this argument is a deep seated belief that something decisive needed to be done because for many years the Justice Department had been pursuing the wrong agenda.

The other side argues that the politics behind the firing is what indicates GWB is an awful president. In these cases, there had been politically motivated behind-the-scenes attempts by the White House to interfere with cases on which the attorneys were working. Their argument is not that the president isn't entitled to fire attorneys, but that the president is not entitled to try to influence the attorneys' actions for his political gain. That is what is wrong. In the end, both sides use a good deal of filtering to see the facts consistent with their view of the president.

What is important here is that we have a lot of opportunity to get the problem wrong. It can be a failure to see the customer's perspective, the assumption that we already understand the problem, the blindness to miss the right point of view altogether, the influence of deep-seated beliefs, and the effect of repeating the old success pattern hundreds of times. What neuroscience seems to suggest is that this shortcoming is not a blameworthy problem. That is, it is important to recognize this is not a conscious behavior, which is why it is so difficult to recognize until after the fact. We often, really are too close to the problem to see it properly.

The Value of Knowledgeable Novices

History and experience suggest that the right novice well placed is sometimes the best way to solve a problem. Novices come at a problem without any of the mental moats the expert is unable to ford.[21] Theoretical physics is a great example. It has long been the domain of the novice. In this context, a novice isn't someone who lacks knowledge, but, rather, someone who has not yet embraced a point of view or repeated a behavior frequently enough to have ossified a brain pattern. Einstein was just such a novice when he published his four landmark papers in 1905. Most of his thinking at that time was done independently although not always alone. He verbalized ideas to others but was often just talking to himself. It was serendipitous that, while working at the patent office, he reviewed a patent application dealing with the transmission of electric signals and electrical-mechanical synchronization of time. These became the fodder for his *thought experiments*, which led to his revolutionary insights into the nature of light and the basic link between space and time. He was a novice in the sense that he'd not adopted a point of view; nevertheless, he was very knowledgeable in his field.

In many fields where synthesis is the key to new knowledge, often it is a novice who delivers the breakthrough. In physics and mathematics, PhDs worry as they approach their thirtieth birthdays that they are rapidly losing the opportunity to come up with something truly revolutionary. The notion is that their brains ossify around the knowledge they have and that limits their ability to see something

---

21 The Novice Supersynthesizer™ is a person who possesses extraordinary problem solving skills but has not absorbed a mindset around the problem at hand.

new. This is true in every human endeavor. We should try to leverage this insight in a business context.

When a business faces a problem, using a novice will bring a fresh perspective. What kind of novice do you want? Preferably you want someone with the capacity to see the big picture and who has good synthesis skills. Perhaps you should use someone with a history of problem solving (as distinct from someone who is just good at project delivery). Find someone with a broad set of curiosities who can easily get sidetracked trying to get to the bottom of something. Find someone with all these characteristics, and you have a good chance at getting a fresh perspective on the problem. Don't be surprised if the experts closest to the problem think the novice has it all wrong. It took about four years for physicists to stop rejecting Einstein's ideas expressed in his four 1905 papers.

FINDING SYNTHESIS TALENT

During WWII, when the B-24 came into the battle, it was better armored than the older B-17. The B-17 crews petitioned to have the B-17 better protected too. To address concerns of the crews, the army initiated a project to retrofit armor on the B-17. Whenever a plane returned damaged from a bombing mission, engineers would note where the plane had been shot and figure out how to better armor those spots. One day, a general was touring the base and, as part of the tour, was taken to where engineers were inspecting a bomber fresh from a mission. As their work was being explained to him, on the other side of the hangar a private who was working on another plane, muttered something under his breath. The general, whose hearing was particularly acute, turned and walked to the private, and said, "Did you say something, private?"

"Well, sir," The private replied, looking cautiously at the general. "I said this plane returned safely from its mission, sir."

For a moment, the general looked at the private, then winked and turned to the engineers.

"Gentlemen, you're beefing up the wrong places."

In this legend, the private understood that crews could usually survive bullets hitting the plane. What they were less likely to survive was a fiery crash. The private saw the bigger picture and was able to understand the problem not as crews want the B-17 to have more armor, but as crews want a better chance of surviving. From that point forward the army placed the armor where a hit might bring a plane down.

How can a company identify people who can synthesize? Who, like our WWII private, can bring such simple clarity to a problem and make its solution obvious? Who can more easily divine patterns that ultimately let them combine patterns from distant knowledge to discover a solution?

Superprogrammer

Jobs that allow a person to clearly demonstrate his or her synthesis talent do exist. An area where this level of synthesis talent becomes evident is in computer programming. It turns out there is a difference between just good computer programming and the more fundamental talent of problem solving. Nevertheless, determining how you're going to get a computer to do something is pure synthesis. In the early days of computer programming, it was noticed that a few programmers were much better than average. This phenomenon generated sufficient interest that several studies of the ability were produced in the 70s and 80s of the last century. What was remarkable was the degree of difference between a good programmer and a superprogrammer. It wasn't that they were a bit better or even twice as productive. The studies showed these programmers were between fourteen times and twenty-eight times better than good programmers. To be fourteen times better than the average expert in any field is amazing.

What a superprogrammer is able to do is completely understand the big picture business problem, see the entire solution in his or her brain, and understand how all the details fit together. This incorporates the ability to look at the problem from different perspectives, like counting rulers. Then, with amazing clarity, he or she quickly writes the computer code to provide the solution. Not only that, but the code is elegant and usually runs error free right from the start. Computer languages, like mathematical axioms, lend themselves to very clear solutions if you know exactly what you want the computer to do. It is a little like putting a jigsaw puzzle together—the pieces really only fit in predetermined ways. The interesting part of the superprogrammer is grasping the business problem, seeing the solution, and then mentally manipulating the computer language to obtain the desired behavior.

A superprogrammer is not interested in doing the documentation, testing, or subsequent maintenance of the program. He or she would be unhappy to have to follow a prescribed programming discipline. He or she wants to create elegant code quickly and move onto the next challenge.

I have had the pleasure of working with two of these superprogrammers in my business life. One supported me in writing a simulator of a large system for a training class. Whenever I would want to make a change to a scenario that required coding, he would ask questions until he understood exactly what was needed, look up at the ceiling in thought for as long as fifteen seconds, then in a few minutes go straight into the existing code, make changes, run the program, and out would come the expected result.

The other fellow I worked with was a very *different* kind of person. Nerds would have called him a nerd. He wasn't as good a communicator, and if he couldn't get the client to fully explain what was needed, he would figure out which ways it could go and write code for these different options. On two occasions, I looked at the screens and suggested we make a change to a user interface; he already had lovely alternatives for me to look at. Occasionally, I saw him ordered to write code in a very specific way. He would comply and also write it the way he thought it should be. His way was always better.

Chief Programmer Team

IBM built a job function around this kind of talent. Others in the industry adopted this concept as well. The job function was called chief programmer team. The superprogrammer was the chief programmer. Also on the team was a librarian, a couple of code documenters, a testing team, and a couple of more *normal* programmers who ended up doing some of the less critical peripheral programming. The chief programmer wrote the core code, and all the other people performed the functions necessary to meet the company's standards for software development. Under this model, IBM and others delivered numerous projects quickly and efficiently.

However, for a number of reasons, this concept is not used much anymore. One of the most interesting stated reasons for this is "because we cannot depend upon the existence of a superprogrammer in any given project."[22] You would think that with a skill this valuable, companies would have gone out and hired as many of these people as they could find, so they'd have enough to meet the need.

---

22 Aron, J.D. *Classics in Software Engineering*, (Upper Saddle River, NJ: Yourdon Press, 1979), 35-39.

Corning Glass Production Engineer

Corning Glass may have been the only company that developed a recruitment and retention plan around this kind of big-picture talent. These were production engineers. Back in the last century, as Corning was expanding internationally, it sought college graduates who were able to see the big picture. Corning needed people who could see how the whole specialty glass-making operation came together, as well as understand the details. The talent they were looking for would allow the company to find solutions to problems where the local environment was more primitive than in the United States. Realizing there were only a few such talented people, Corning sought to find and hire them before other companies recognized their importance. As it turns out, they seemed to be alone in the ability to recognize this pivotal talent.

Chief Design Engineer

For years, whenever they were launching a new type of plane, Boeing also used this type of talent in the role of chief design engineer. The company saw the value of having someone in that role who had the capacity to understand how the whole plane came together. That is someone who understood how design changes in one area could affect the airframe, avionics, flight controls, engines, APU, hydraulics, etc. The chief design engineer could minimize the impact of a change in one area by realizing early on that a design change in another system was needed.

In the case of the 787 airplanes, Boeing has distributed not just the manufacturing of components but also the design. As a consequence, when the third party solves problems before delivery, no one at Boeing is involved. It is impossible to have someone playing the role of chief design engineer today with that depth of understanding, because design and design changes are no longer centralized. With all the delays of the 787 Dreamliner, Boeing has said that the company may go back to its practice of supplying complete designs, rather than asking third party suppliers to do design work as it did with the 787. As Peter Drucker observed, "The most efficient way to produce anything is to bring together under one management as many as possible of the activities needed to turn out the product."[23] Of course, the other risk for Boeing is the forfeiture of innovative knowledge in the form of know-how. Know-how develops as you start to build something and unanticipated difficulties arise and are resolved. Under Boeing's strategy, third parties will hold that knowledge, so it is easier for competitors to take advantage of the innovation.

Supersynthesizers™

People with this extraordinary synthesis talent exist in every type of job. They are not just computer programmers, engineers, and theoretical physicists; those fields just allow individuals to show off their talents more easily. In other fields, this talent is often difficult to detect.

On a business trip into Dubai, I had the pleasure of working with a quiet gentleman from South Asia. Based on his passion for problem

---

23 http://www.saidwhat.co.uk/quotes/favourite/peter_f_drucker, Accessed 12/1/2009

solving, his broad knowledge, and his extraordinary curiosity, I suspected he was a supersynthesizer. Later, I put him on a problem-solving team working on updating one of our core systems. His ability to see the big picture and how the pieces fit together took us well outside the scope of the assignment and helped change our business model. The change was credited with the ability to drive $2 billion in incremental annual sales!

The clear value of the supersynthesizer talent suggests that astute business leaders would have HR departments developing talent management activities to find and develop these capabilities in individuals. However, it turns out that not only is this talent fairly rare, but it is also hard to identify. Even in the field of computer programming, it is not easy to identify supersynthesizing talent. A fairly large number of programmers can quickly produce lots of code that is beautifully written and runs perfectly. Unfortunately, if the programmer did not really understand the business problem—the big picture or how all the detail fit together—his code would only approximate solving the underlying business problem. This can be a subtle problem and not immediately recognized. Here, the programmer is an accomplished technician, but not a synthesizer who understands the big picture and how the solution must fit together to meet the business need.

Hiding the Talent

Another difficulty in identifying this kind of talent is that we typically identify people's capabilities based on knowledge and performance. Knowledge is evaluated in terms of formal education and experience. Much of the knowledge a supersynthesizer absorbs comes from the perimeter and is not going to show up as part of his college degree or work experience. Supersynthesizers tend to be deeply curious and absorb knowledge in unconventional ways. This deep curiosity is one of the best indicators of the utility of a person with synthesis talent.

Performance is how well you did against goals. Many companies like to think they are good at setting clear, objective, measurable goals. The trouble with setting goals like that is that most people can figure out ways to exceed them. This should be a good thing, but many companies use some sort of forced ranking systems that undermines the usefulness of clear, measurable goals. In the end, performance is not judged solely on objective criteria. There are soft judgments made on how well you work on the team, how good your business savvy is, whether you think well on your feet, how much you know about sports, whether others like you, how good your golf game is…and so on. Yes, it is odd to think that things like sports knowledge and how much others like you matter. These kinds of factors influence personal judgments about how well people fit into the workplace. Bias plays a subtle but very real role in making these judgments. As we will see below, on the soft judgments, including measures of emotional intelligence (EI), a supersynthesizer is likely to score poorly.

Kirton

Personality profiles like the Kirton Adaption-Innovation Inventory (KAI) do not measure synthesis talent, although Kirton does propose to ask questions that predict where you're likely to fall on the change continuum. That is, are you more comfortable with making changes within the existing structure, which Kirton calls an *adaptor* or are you an *innovator* and more inclined to completely change the structure itself?

The Tale of a Pig

The villagers of Innovatorburg and the more numerous townspeople of Adaptorville were fighting over the last remaining hog in the forest. It was an old, tame pig loved by the Adaptors and liked but not loved by the Innovators. Suddenly, as one group tugged the poor pig by the ears toward their village, and the other group pulled it in the opposite direction by the tail, the tail popped off. The more numerous Adaptors immediately seized the now defective pig and claimed it.

Along came a magic ointment salesman. "Ah, this is not problem," said the salesman. "I have a potion that will grow back the missing bit."

The Adaptors immediately bought the potion and applied a dab to the rear of the pig. BOING!! Suddenly, there was a new, beautiful curly tail—clearly the most beautiful part of the pig. The Adaptors were very happy, and off they strode, pig in tow, toward their village.

The sad Innovators picked up the discarded potion bottle and applied a generous portion to the end of the tail. BOING!! Suddenly, a new hog popped on to the old tail. This young energetic hog immediately took off running and dancing toward the trees, with the Innovators wildly chasing after it.

Generally, adaptors are more comfortable taking the current system, product, or offering, and changing just a bit of it. The innovators, on the other hand, want to throw out most of the old bits and start fresh.

Myers-Briggs

Myers-Briggs Talent Inventory (MBTI) also doesn't specifically attempt to identify this synthesis skill. (See below on the correlation between Myers-Briggs and Kirton.) Additionally, there is a company in Michigan that claims great success in using a variation of the Myers-Briggs test to identify innovation talent.

Interesting conclusions have come out of studies comparing Myers-Briggs Talent Inventory (MBTI) and Kirton Adaptor Innovator (KAI) inventory. Most innovators are NTPs or iNtuition, Thinking, and Perception. The highest correlation between MBTI and KAI was that innovators were Intuitives.[1]

In studying senior corporate managers, it turns out that a huge majority of their Myers-Briggs profiles are STJs or Sensing, Thinking, and Feeling.[1]

The significance of these studies is that corporate leaders are sensors and innovators are Intuitives. This creates a couple of areas of major disconnect between management and problem solvers.

Senior managers (Sensors) tend to be more comfortable with improving existing structures and changes within the scope of existing products, processes, systems, and technologies. Problem solvers (Intuitives) are very comfortable with substantive change.

Sensors tend to see threats and opportunities inside the existing company and within existing product lines, business models, and existing competitors. Intuitives are more likely to see threats and opportunities outside the company and beyond existing business models, competitors, and products.

Sensors tend to feel a stronger need to conform to rules and procedures, whereas Intuitives feel the rules and procedures must change along with everything else.

Sensors would likely describe themselves as practical. Intuitives are far more likely to do something because they believe it is the right thing to do.

A significant problem is in communication. Management, as a group of STJs, may share common understandings and assume that everyone else shares this same point of view, and it isn't necessary to communicate it. Likewise, Innovators may perceive something as simple to do, when management thinks it is risky. As a consequence, innovators may fail to keep management adequately informed.

The biggest risk is for Sensors to discount the potential contribution of the Intuitives.

Hammering a nail is a skill, just as synthesis is a skill. You wouldn't use a questionnaire like Myers-Briggs or KAI to choose a carpenter to hammer nails. Asking the carpenter to demonstrate nail-hammering skills would decide the matter. Likewise, synthesis is a demonstrable skill. In our work, we've developed a tool that can help an individual demonstrate his or her synthesis skill.

Why use any tool to identify great problem solvers? Surely it is obvious who is and who isn't a great problem solver. Several factors account for the fact that this is false. One factor is mistaking a strong implementation person for a strong problem solver.

An important business unit in a large bank had an individual who was highly regarded as a person who could deliver solutions on time and in budget nearly 100 percent of the time. When you had a problem, you presented it, along with your solution to him, and he would determine if your solution would be implemented. However, over time, the business unit delivered no significant changes to product, process, or systems. It had been very good at delivering small and, as it turned out, insignificant changes.

The reason for this was simple: the individual who'd become the de facto gatekeeper had a delivery reputation to maintain. Any change that was difficult or had some risk of failure was blocked at project initiation. Projects that did have some risk and had senior management backing were either watered down to make them less risky, or the gatekeeper made himself unavailable to work the project. The business unit was very happy with its problem-solving capability, its change process, and its success rate. They were stumped as to why they failed to keep pace with other industry leaders. They looked at every external factor but were blind to the internal cause. It was simple to see from the outside— innovations are risky, and they were not delivering innovations.

Her Ideas Are Absurd

It turns out it is much trickier to identify exceptional problem solvers than simply making the mistake of thinking a good delivery person is a good problem solver. Einstein captured the problem succinctly when he said, "If at first the idea is not absurd, there is no hope for it." The failure to recognize a idea is legendary. In 1943, Tom Watson, CEO of IBM at the time, famously said, "I think there is a world market for about five computers." Or take Ken Olson, CEO of Digital, who dismissed the notion of personal computers saying, "There is no reason for any individual to have a computer in his home."

Gary Starkweather was ordered to stop working on the laser printer when he worked for Xerox in Rochester, New York, but he pursued it anyway. Later, after its success as a mainframe printer, he wanted to build a small one for personal use, but the powers at Xerox forbade him, saying there was only a market for around 300 units. As a result, HP developed the personal laser printer, sold millions of them, and took ownership of that market instead of Xerox.

When asked to evaluate Fred Smith's idea for FedEx delivery service, a Yale University professor dismissed it and said, "The concept is interesting and well-formed, but in order to earn better than a C, the idea must be feasible."

President McKnight of 3M told Dick Drew to drop his little personal project and get back to work on improving sandpaper. Drew famously ignored his chief and completed the development of masking tape, which became one of 3M's leading products.

This incident eventually led 3M to adopt the mantra If you have the right person on the right project, and they are absolutely dedicated to finding a solution—leave them alone. Tolerate their initiative and trust them.

We've hundreds of examples in the innovation literature of this type of response. This should surprise none of us. John Funk, a principal at Evergreen Innovation Partners, has heard just about every reason why an idea won't work or why a business won't succeed. His personal favorite stupid reason is "the competition would have done this already if it was such a great idea." Solutions that look obvious in hindsight often look ridiculous in foresight and vice-versa.

Einstein was right; great ideas seem absurd at first. It is a fundamental problem we deal with as humans. It isn't that we are threatened by change, although some people are more susceptible to that response. It's that our brains create this conundrum. The brain makes repeated neural patterns stronger and more rigid. It limits our ability to see alternatives to that behavior and the ideas behind it. What is a little frightening is how certain we are that the new idea is stupid. Later, once we have changed our minds, we cannot imagine what we were thinking.

When I presented the idea to change the business model that the gentleman from Dubai had helped us develop, our chairman's reaction was similar. He thought the idea was stupid. A couple of weeks went by before he changed his mind and became a strong advocate for the change.

Supersynthesizers come up with lots of *crazy* ideas, and this creates the perception that this person is way out there, so we don't pay too much attention to what he or she says. Then, when good fortune shines, and the company implements one of these ideas, the solution is obvious in hindsight, which discounts the value of both the idea and the contribution of the person who originated it. Most of us have heard about some successful new idea and said to ourselves "I could have thought of that."

Why do we have this initial response to good ideas? We've already pointed out, in the context of seeing a problem correctly, that established patterns get in the way. Exactly the same thing happens when we first hear good ideas. Our brains develop rigid patterns around often-repeated success behaviors, and we interpret new data to fit it into the established patterns.

Neuroscience now suggests that our ability to be influenced, to change our mind, is related to the brain's elasticity. A behavior like the rat running the maze more than 200 times, or the human performing the identical process year in and year out, creates a very inelastic synaptic pattern that is not susceptible to influence. Like concrete, which starts fluid and sets hard, the mind also sets hard. This is what the term *mindset* refers to—a fixed mental attitude.

A gentleman from central Europe went to northern California and, hearing about the bear country up in the Trinity Alps, decided to go up there for some hunting. Being a self-styled outdoorsman, he declined a guide and set out on his own on a bright clear morning in search of bear. By noon, clouds had rolled in, and it had started to snow. At three in the afternoon, the gentleman admitted to himself with a touch of panic that he might be a bit lost. He thought the village he sought was off to his left somewhat. He began to walk through the snow bearing slightly left. He went up and then down, and then up again. After a time he'd unknowingly made a circle and was greatly relieved to find tracks in the snow. Figuring whoever had left these fresh tracks must know where he was going, he followed them.

After a little while, a third set of tracks joined, and then a fourth. He was greatly encouraged with the fifth and six, especially as it looked like darkness would fall soon. All of a sudden, he came upon a local woodsman.

"I've been watching you," said the woodsman. "If you're looking for the village, it is just down at the bottom of this hill here, on the other side of that thick stand of pine."

Being suspicious of strangers, the European gentleman thanked the woodsman but announced that he would stick to the well-worn trail. And off he trod. In a while a seventh and then an eighth set of tracks had joined. But it was getting quite dark. Then, suddenly, he noticed down the hill a set of lights. Being very tired and hungry he decided to abandon the trail and head for the lights.

There he found the village and made his way to the tavern. Once inside, he saw the woodsman at the bar and walked up to him. "Thought you'd get the best of me back there a few miles, eh? Well I'm no fool," he said and headed for a table.

In a business context, this is important because the same phenomenon occurs. We can end up "following our own footsteps." A frequently repeated process, pitch, product, or management practice creates a point of view. As the psychologist Edward Tolman showed, this happens irrespective of the longevity of the success of the behavior. Repetition reinforces it. Our brains limit our susceptibility to influence around change.

Chances are at some point in your work life you watched someone push a change that is now perceived as obviously necessary and correct but at the time met a lot of resistance. This is because our brains create a rigid structure around a successful behavior. This mental ossification is a natural function of how the brain processes memories to select successful patterns and behaviors. Because they are successful, the brain selects them as the guide for future behavior. If it didn't have such a regulator, then we'd be experimenting endlessly and failing most of the time.

As we age, proteins in the eye cause a gradual reduction in the elasticity of the lens. Our vision deteriorates, and we need glasses to read. We may also require stronger prescriptions to see distances. This loss of lens elasticity provides a metaphor for what happens to the elasticity of the brain. The brain changes with age. The groves (Sulci) on the surface of the brain widen, and the voids in the brain containing cerebrospinal fluid expand with age. As we get older, the brain also becomes smaller in both weight and volume. The bad news for younger people is that this all starts in the mid-20s.

The Elasticity of the Brain

For a long time, neuroscience believed that the loss of elasticity in our brains caused by aging was unavoidable. Researchers at MIT's Picower found that mice with atrophied brains similar to those of Alzheimer's patients regained long-term memories and the ability to learn after living in a more stimulating environment. Specifically, the enriched environment enhanced both the physical and psychological well being of the mice. When exposed to the enriched environment, the brain cells in these mice began to sprout new connections. Elsewhere, research indicates that people who use their brains to learn something completely new also regain brain elasticity. However, this brain exercise has to *stretch* the brain in new ways. Perhaps if you are fluent in Spanish, studying Portuguese is not a sufficient stretch, since the two languages are very similar. Maybe studying calculus or the art of basket weaving would be more stimulating for your brain. But studying Portuguese would be much better than studying nothing at all.

This notion of stretching the brain with new knowledge is important to any company wishing to become the innovative competitor in its industry. Not only does the pursuit of knowledge help keep the brain elastic, but it enhances the ability of people to solve problems. In the last chapter, we talked of the value knowledge brings synthesizers like Feynman who draw from broad knowledge to provide the framework of patterns, the metaphors, that provide solutions to problems.

Unwanted Solutions and Low Emotional Intelligence (EQ)

Thus we have this wonderful innovative talent, the supersynthesizer ability, which is not going to jump off the page in any of the ways companies evaluate talent. It is also not going to be recognized for its idea production since most ideas are a bit crazy, and the ideas that do get implemented seem like obvious solutions. Moreover, two other factors inhibit a company's ability to identify this talent. The first is that the people who have this talent often end up hiding it. Second, people with this talent often have underdeveloped social skills.

Creative innovators (supersynthesizers) *are passionate about problem solving*. They see problems even where others don't, and they also have solutions to those unwanted problems. This inclination to point out problems where others don't see the problems generally does not serve the innovator well. People have enough important problems not to be bothered by these less obvious problems. In other words, the behavior is not met with welcoming arms.

Robert Sutton points out that most creative innovators share certain characteristics. In many business settings, these characteristics are liabilities.

Innovators don't have much respect for authority. From their perspective, the value is not in *who* said it, but *what* was said. This is an obvious problem in a hierarchical organization where the value of the thinking is established based on the rank of the speaker and not on its content.

They tend to be low self-monitors. That is, they are not very adept or don't pay attention to nonverbal communication signals—body language. This is not a constant weakness, but unfortunately pops up whenever they get wrapped up in talking about some difficult problem or great solution. Their focus is on the facts not the feelings. Just when it is most important and useful in a corporate setting to demonstrate high emotional intelligence, the problem solver shows none at all.

Innovators can also *project* the wrong signals. For example, an innovator is struggling to communicate an idea to her peers and says to herself, "Come on, don't be stupid. Figure out a way to get this across." Unfortunately, the thought is accompanied by the facial expression that goes along with "don't be stupid." The unconscious facial expression has an unintended effect on her audience. Assuming it's directed at them, they get angry. From that point forward, the quality of the idea is inconsequential; communication has broken down, and our innovator is completely oblivious of her error.

The same can be true of verbal communication, as a story in Richard Feynman's *What Do You Care What Other People Think* makes clear. He had been nominated to the task force to investigate the Space Shuttle Challenger disaster in 1986. He was neither comfortable with his role nor happy about working in Washington, D.C. After a few weeks on the task force and feeling like the odd man out, a new member joined the group, a physicist named Dr. Keel.

> When he introduced himself on Monday, he joked that the last 'honest work' he had done for a living was some aerodynamics work for the shuttle program ten or twelve years ago. So I felt very comfortable with him. Well, I haven't been talking to Dr. Keel for more than five minutes, when he tells me he's never been so insulted in his life, that he didn't take this job to be so insulted, and that he doesn't want to talk to me anymore!...I was very surprised by his reaction. I had undoubtedly said some boorish, brash damn fool thing, which I therefore can't remember![24]

This exchange bothered Dr. Feynman and he later tried to piece together what he might have said:

> Now, Dr. Keel started out by telling me that he had a degree in physics. I always assumed that everybody in physics has integrity—perhaps I'm naive about that—so I must have asked him a question I often think about: 'how can a man of integrity get along in Washington?' It's very easy to read that question another way: 'since you're getting along in Washington, you can't be a man of integrity!'[25]

---

24 R.P. Feynman, R. Leighton. What Do You Care What Other People Think?: Further Adventures of a Curious Character. W.W. Norton & Company, New York, (1988) p, 162
25 Ibid., p. 218

Feynman's accident is characteristic of the kind of behavior that can so easily be misunderstood. It was not Feynman's nature to insult anyone, much less someone he had just met and liked. Low self-monitors are prone to this sort of problem. Because they are oblivious to emotional nuance in verbal and nonverbal signals, they can often get into very deep trouble before they realize it. And, by the time they do, too much inadvertent damage has been done.

As companies are now starting to focus on emotional intelligence, they risk blinding themselves to the fundamental reality that super-synthesizers will often have low emotional intelligence:

> Of course, the opposite of high EI is not difficult to rec-ognize. If you are exposed to a co-worker who...has little or no sensitivity to the feelings of others, that co-worker's communications often tend to hurt or antag-onize others. As more and more companies perceive their dependence on good teaming among employ-ees and on earning the goodwill of customers who will not tolerate rudeness, these companies are both seek-ing workers with high EI and implementing training to improve the emotional intelligence skills of existing employees.[26]

This training idea is a fool's errand. It would be far more produc-tive to train those with high emotional intelligence to learn to lead creative people. The truth is the hurtful communication is almost

---

26 R. Fitzgerald, Emotional Intelligence, SuccessInTeaching.info, accessed 11/13/2009, http://www.successinteaching.info/SuccessInTeaching/Emotional_Intelligence.html.

always unintentional. An adult who's achieved adulthood as a low self-monitor is going to be very difficult to convert into a high self-monitor.

First of all, many high self-monitors don't really believe the low self-monitor is unable to detect the nonverbal signals. The signals are so obvious to them that they believe the low self-monitor's oblivious behavior is deliberate. The training often assumes this is true. I sat in on a session designed to help people like this become more influential. The material in the course often suggested things like "pay attention to the other person. When you notice they are uncomfortable then…" That advice assumes everyone has this capability to read these signals.

Second, high self-monitors often do not realize how subtle differences in facial expressions can be. If you've reached adulthood without learning this, it is very difficult to learn or to teach. It is like learning a new language, where the alphabet is alien, the sounds are alien, and the whole thing seems to lack structure. Moreover, low self-monitors will not likely see the return as worth the investment. After all, they often live by Feynman's credo: What do you care what other people think?

Another important and relevant characteristic of supersynthesizers is that *they tend to prefer to work out a solution alone.* They want to be able to think a problem through, do very targeted research, and get to the best possible solution as quickly as possible. Other people are very useful in getting research questions answered and talking through ideas. However, their feelings are seen as irrelevant.

Feynman: Soloist

Earlier, I mentioned that Richard Feynman had been picked to participate on the Manhattan Project because of his strong problem-solving
skills. This was the reason he was chosen for the Rogers commission
on the Challenger disaster. Rightly or wrongly, in the end, Feynman
was credited with discovering the cold weather O-ring problem on
the Challenger.

He was a physicist not an engineer and didn't know much about
the Space Shuttle or the Challenger accident. So to get the knowledge
needed to understand the problem, he met with the most knowledgeable Space Shuttle engineers. Before going to Washington, D.C., he
visited the Jet Propulsion Laboratory (JPL) nearby his Santa Barbara
home. He described it this way:

> It's called a briefing, but it wasn't brief: it was very in-
> tense, very fast, and very complete. It's the only way I
> know to get technical information quickly: you don't
> just sit there while they go through what they think
> would be interesting; instead, you ask a lot of ques-
> tions, you get quick answers, and soon you begin to
> understand the circumstances and learn just what to
> ask to get the next piece of information you need.

In the first two lines of his notes from that meeting is the cause
of the disaster, hot gases burning past the O-rings in booster rocket
joints. Feynman engaged the engineers at the JPL, not for their help
in creating a solution, but for their knowledge that would later help
Feynman uncover the problem.

Generally supersynthesizers don't care for teams. The trouble with teams, from their perspective, is that they often go off in search of answers to questions the problem solver sees as irrelevant. Or worse, the team starts acting like a committee and spends lots of time figuring out how often they will meet, comparing calendars, setting up rules of the committee, establishing a list of milestones, time frames, document formats, and so on. All this is long before the problem is well defined or any solutions have been proposed. The problem solver just wants to get to work on the problem.

The day after the JPL briefing, Feynman was in Washington ready to go to work. The first meeting was all administrative stuff about how the work was to be organized, who was going to do the writing, how the press was going to be dealt with, etc. The next day was the public meeting, with the press and big cheese from NASA present. Of course, it soon became apparent that the Commission was not prepared to answer any technical questions and instead promised "to get that information to you later." The next day they met privately for just two hours, and the day after that, they held another public meeting with more promises "to get that information to you later." Feynman was champing at the bit to dig into the real issues but discovered that he would have nothing to do until the next commission meeting five days later in Florida. In exasperation, he nearly quit. Eventually, he did go off on his own to talk to the technical experts. In the end, Feynman was the person who brought the accident cause to the Commission.

In the corporate environment good problem solvers cannot usually go off on their own, abandoning the team to work the way they find most effective. However, that is exactly how masking tape, Post-It Notes, the laser printer, and thousands of breakthrough ideas were pursued.

Hubris

Finally, great problem solvers, like other creative people, can be cursed with an abundance of hubris. Wolfgang Pauli was a physicist who had this affliction in spades. Victor Weisskopf, a student of Pauli's and later a famous physicist in his own right, recalls discovering an error in one of his own published calculations. He asked Pauli if he should give up physics.

"Don't," Pauli responded. "Everyone makes mistakes. Except me."

Once in 1931, Pauli was attending a Robert Oppenheimer lecture. Oppenheimer had written equations filling the blackboard. Suddenly, and without warning, Pauli ran up to the blackboard and completely erased it. He put the eraser down and announced, "Nonsense!" He didn't feel any need to explain further.

Here was a fellow with way too much hubris. Right below hubris on the spectrum is ample self-confidence without the same degree of arrogance. Feynman had great self-confidence. When he worked on the Manhattan project, Neils Bohr liked to bounce ideas off the much younger Feynman because Feynman was not awed by him. Feynman's confidence was such that he could have a frank discussion with any physicist, regardless of stature. Neils Bohr appreciated that he could talk for hours with Feynman and get honest peer-to-peer input from a young man who'd yet to make a recognized or substantial contribution to the field of physics.

Supersynthesizers have great self-confidence in their problem-solving abilities. That, coupled with their inadvertent failure to discern nonverbal communication signals, often causes them to come across as arrogant. This can get in the way of management being willing to put them in positions where they represent the department on an innovation team.

We have discussed that problem solving often isn't something that gets identified through the way companies measure performance. And knowledge is evaluated based on what formal education a person has. And the type of knowledge that's valued is knowledge related specifically to the expertise required for the job. As a result, supersynthesizers often aren't recognized or valued in the business world. Perhaps the single biggest obstacle to innovation is that great ideas are often labeled crazy and tossed aside.

History's Lesson

In Medieval Europe the Church exercised supreme power. Then, along came Galileo.

Galileo could see Jupiter's moons rotating around Jupiter, and with the help of Kepler, he could describe that rotation mathematically. The validity of the applied mathematics could be verified by observation. The same formulas worked for calculating the moon's rotation around the earth and the rotation of the earth around the sun. Galileo made his claim that the earth was not the center of the solar system and ran afoul of the Roman Catholic Church.

For its part, the Church did itself no favors by denouncing Galileo's demonstration of a heliocentric solar system. Because this was both observable and mathematically sound, the veracity of the Church's *authority* came into question.

Galileo's discovery provided the crack that secular rulers needed to wrestle power from the Church. The old rigid hierarchy began to erode. This allowed a deeper inquiry into the true nature of the world. Research became routine, and research, through discovery, experimentation, and synthesis, produced new knowledge.

The Devil's in the Hierarchy

The secular state's support of nondogmatic sources of knowledge and the application of scientific method made possible the Industrial Revolution, which took off in England in the nineteenth century. The biggest obstacle to innovation is the entrenched authority that the hierarchy allows to develop.

In the modern corporate environment, often the hierarchical nature of the organization works against the freedom to think. The value of a thought is determined by how high in the organization the thinker is. Hierarchy becomes all about authority not leadership. Likewise, moving an idea from thinking to development becomes less likely if the idea's originator is way down the hierarchy. This means that many good ideas never gain traction. The solution in Kanter's story about the yarn-breaking problem came from the factory floor. Had the idea been born of a higher class, it would have been implemented much sooner. Hierarchy is an insidious problem in a company.

In his best seller, *Good to Great,* Jim Collins suggests that hierarchy not only works against creative thought but can also work against achieving the growth and income potential of the company. Organizations boasting a powerful hierarchy may be the worst places for supersynthesizers to work. Where the value of an idea is determined by how high its originator is in the organization, the likelihood of good problem solvers achieving their potential is very low. Experience has shown that hierarchy provides more utility to the self-aggrandizers who thrive on power and status than it does the company's stockholders.

Hierarchy serves two purposes. One is to enable the allocation of resources and provide a way to come to decisions—this is the corporate and stockholder's purpose. If this purpose is not held to, the second purpose can emerge. Here, the emerging purposes are the selfish aims of those seeking power and prestige. The hierarchy only changes subtly. Structurally, it looks the same, but functionally, it mutates.

This catalogue of things that get in the way of identifying and leveraging the great problem-solving skills of internal synthesizers combine to impede a company's ability to be a competitive leader. Companies that deal with these issues will make themselves much stronger competitors. In the final chapter, I will talk about how to deal with these issues and how to utilize supersynthesizers, super problem solvers in a business. Before we leave the topic of talent, we need to talk a little about the role of knowledge.

Being able to synthesize and being able to see the big picture, as well as all the details, is crucial to defining the problem. Actually, the talent goes beyond just the ability to define a problem—often it's more important to be able to find the problem in the first place. The problem can be subtle until exposed, like the private pointing out the armor objective of the B-17 crews or the pipeline engineer seeing the problem not as the pipe bending but as air pockets forming.

Understanding the problem is the bulk of the work. I spoke with a former innovation manager for Proctor and Gamble who said that, after a career of innovation, he realized that his most successful projects were the ones where he spent 95 percent of his time defining the problem and 5 percent solving it. Likewise, Einstein is reported to have said, "If I had an hour to save the world, I would spend fifty-nine minutes defining the problem and one minute finding solutions."

Broad Knowledge Is Valuable

What enables a great problem solver to focus the bulk of his or her effort on defining the problem is his or her ability to easily find a solution. Defining the problem creates the right mental patterns representing the problem in your brain. Then, your brain has the best opportunity for coming up with a solution whose pattern matches the patterns of the problem. However, the source of those solutions is the knowledge already present in the person's brain. While problem solvers often cannot explain where the solution came from and cannot identify the specific knowledge that provided the pattern, it is clear that broad knowledge plays that key role.

Great synthesizers in history had tremendous curiosity and a willingness to pursue the exploration to new knowledge. Newton, Einstein,

Feynman, Descartes, Galileo, and Edison were all men of great intellectual curiosity, with the drive to dig for knowledge and go where no one had gone before.

The people who can contribute the most brainpower and breadth of knowledge to problem solving and innovation are supersynthesizers. These are people who've trained the right side of their brains to make use of distant and unprecedented connections and filled that brain space with knowledge patterns from broad sources. Companies that are great at innovating find ways to leverage this small, valuable talent pool.

THE G.O.L.F. T.E.E.™
CEO

Gʀᴇᴀᴛ Oʀɢᴀɴɪᴢᴀᴛɪᴏɴᴀʟ Lᴇᴀᴅᴇʀsʜɪᴘ Fᴏsᴛᴇʀs: Tʀᴜsᴛ, Eɴɢᴀɢᴇᴍᴇɴᴛ, ᴀɴᴅ Eᴍᴘᴏᴡᴇʀᴍᴇɴᴛ.

The Golf Tee makes it easy to remember Trust, Engage, Empower

The one thing a CEO can clearly take credit for is the level of innovation the company enjoys. The CEO has incredible leverage to build an innovation engine within the ranks of his or her company. In this chapter we will talk about how a CEO can build this capability. In talks I give to CEOs, I suggest this is tremendously satisfying because it is measurable. The measurement gives the CEO and the Board a clear indicator of the impact the CEO has on the bottom line of the business. Nothing else a CEO does will be as satisfying.

Before taking a single step in the G.OL.F. T.E.E.™ process, the CEO should call for a business forecast for the next twenty-four months. This should be a normal budget forecast. It should not anticipate any G.OL.F. T.E.E.™ results. The point of the forecast is to predict the future of business as it is managed today.

Then let people proceed as they normally would to deliver against forecast. As CEO, however, you are going to implement some minor changes to the way the company works as we describe here as G.OL.F. T.E.E.™ fulcrum points.

Having the desire to make change is, of course, necessary. But it is not sufficient. The CEO must have the know-how to execute the change. When faced with a problem the know-how isn't always obvious, as in the famous story below:

> Ralph Waldo Emerson was a learned man. He'd studied philosophy, science, history, literature, and art. But none of them were particularly helpful when he found himself trying to push a calf into the barn with his son. The two of them pushed from the rear, pulled from the front, grabbed tail and ears alike. Progress was imperceptible. The best evidence that work was being done were their red faces and perspiration soaked shirts. The calf remained unmoved. Then, along came a servant girl. She grinned and stuck a finger in the calf's mouth. The calf, seduced by this maternal proxy, followed her straight into the barn. Emerson smiled at his son and said, "I like people who know how to get things done!"

The G.OL.F. T.E.E. fulcrum points will poise the company to take off with high levels of problem solving and innovation. Each fulcrum point amounts to a small change. Over time they accumulate and produce remarkable change. Nevertheless, it will take at least six months for the fulcrum points to begin to produce noticeable change, but as people begin to trust, and they see empowerment is real, then engagement will take hold. Engaged people will solve problems that will drive profits beyond budget. We will get to the fulcrum points shortly.

At the end of the budgetted twenty-four months, the CEO can comfortably take credit for the lift of profit above budget because it will be due to the CEO's leadership. Moreover, the satisfaction comes not just from the bottom-line improvements but also the engagement and empowerment of employees. People who are engaged and empowered are generally healthier and happier than people who are not. The CEO has changed the world for the people he or she leads. This is a badge of satisfaction the CEO will carry around for his or her lifetime. It's like hitting a hole-in-one, where the value is not so much on today's scorecard, but in the status of joining that most elite echelon in golf.

A McKinsey study in 2008[27] showed that a strong performance on innovation depends on trust and engagement, and that bureaucratic, hierarchical, and fearful environments will inhibit innovation. It is the culture that matters. This is nothing new. The idea that culture is critical to innovation is the single most common theme found in books about innovation.

---

27   J. Barsh, et al, "Leadership and Innovation," *McKinsey Quarterly.com* (January 2008). Accessed 11/13/2009 http://www.mckinseyquarterly.com/Strategy/Innovation/Leadership_and_innovation_2089

The same McKinsey study found that the vast majority of executives are not confident in their ability to stimulate innovation. What is important to recognize is that engagement is the key, but it depends on an environment of trust and empowerment. The source of discomfort for executives lies, not in their ability to instill trust, but rather in their fear of the chaos that could ensue if their people are empowered. What if employees pursue wild, crazy, or stupid ideas as they go off to solve whatever problems they dream up? The question is, how do you control an empowered workforce? The answer is found in the methods and tools you use to facilitate empowerment. We will get to those shortly. The point is, you must empower the workforce to engage them because only engaged employees are going to produce the level of problem solving needed in the *new normal*.

Problem solving is the key to competitive advantage. Without the CEO's intentional leadership, innovation and problem solving will not flourish. The key to problem solving is found in the brain of each employee in the company. To leverage this marvelous resource, you need engaged people who work in an environment of empowerment and trust. Employee **T**rust, **E**ngagement, and **E**mpowerment (TEE)[28] are the essential ingredients. The CEO leads through three actions:

---

28 The full acronym is G.O.L.F. T.E.E. stands for **G**reat **O**rganizational **L**eaders **F**acilitate **T**rust, **E**ngagement, and **E**mpowerment. The three words that matter are **T**rust, **E**ngagement and **E**mpowerment.

Three Tees

Mixed well, the three will create a boundary-pushing, questioning, problem-solving, risk-taking, innovative, productive workforce—a workforce held in awe by the marketplace. Given the right goals and resources, a workforce like this can provide ideas and implementations that deliver the competitive advantage we all seek.

The CEO has the main leadership responsibility to build and maintain an environment that nurtures that workforce. If you are going to run a good problem-solving company, you must be good at creating employee Trust, Engagement, and Empowerment. This requires leadership—not management.

Great CEO leadership isn't about being soft. Great CEOs set high standards. They are tenacious and persistent. The great CEO pays attention to detail and focuses on efficiency. Such a CEO demands deep thinking and clear-headed analysis. A great leader gets the people he or she leads to set high standards for themselves, to be persistent, to think deeply for themselves, to thoroughly analyze, to pay attention to detail, to be efficient, and to always strive for excellence.

First-rate CEOs see this responsibility as their primary responsibility. Second-rate CEOs spend the bulk of their time managing. They are busy making decisions and evaluating performance, trying to figure out how to motivate their subordinates. They see their "value add" is making choices and allocating resources. They believe they should be measured on the outcomes of those choices. Frequently, second-tier CEOs spend no time at all working their T.E.E. responsibilities. At their best, they only give lip service to these crucial responsibilities. They are managers, and managers try to get the most out of their employees. Leaders give their colleagues the opportunity to *be* their best. A good manager is successful, but a good leader is extraordinarily successful.

Command and Control

CEOs who rely on a command environment fail to see they are undermining their ability to maximize performance. These managers can get results too. Command structures work to deliver what needs to be delivered, which is usually what the management thinks is needed, but not always.

> A new lieutenant arrived at the post and commanded the men to form up.
>
> "Men," he said. "I expect only one thing from you. We will get along fine provided you follow my orders to the letter." He surveyed the men. "Is that CLEAR?"
>
> "SIR, YES SIR!" replied the men.
>
> Three weeks later he approached a private. "Private Johnson. Look at the tires on the trucks," he said. "Do they look a little low to you, private?"
>
> "Ah, yes, sir, they are indeed low, sir."
>
> "Didn't I instruct you to check the pressure in the tires every day, private?"
>
> "You did, sir. I even wrote down what the pressure was each day!"
>
> "Then pray tell me, why are the tires nearly flat?"
>
> "Well, sir," replied Johnson. "Every time I check the tires using the tire pressure gauge a little air escapes. After a while, I guess it adds up, sir."

What command structures fail to do is to actualize to the potential. Command structures leave a private accurately performing a stupid task or a factory worker frustrated, stuck for years on an idea to fix a yarn-breaking problem.

General Wesley Clark accidentally discovered this problem with command. When he worked at the U.S. Army's National Training

Center, he observed that the incoming battalions never beat the resident "enemy," and he wondered why. By observing the fighting, he realized that the resident enemy reacted and fought at the individual soldier level. For the visiting army, all the strategy and tactics were managed through the chain of command. The frontline lieutenants were given a set of tactical instructions and expected to execute the tasks as commanded. The soldiers just followed whatever reasonable orders were given.

The training center's resident enemy received no such detailed tactical instruction. Their job was simple: to defeat the incoming army by whatever means necessary. It was the initiative and ingenuity of the frontline soldier that made the difference in the outcome of the battle. The frontline soldiers worked in small teams, defined the problem they faced at any moment, and invented a solution. They were free to behave as thinking adults. That is why the smaller resident enemy always won the battle.

What General Clark realized what that the actions of senior commanders could lose a battle, but their orders could not win it.[29] The incoming army was relying on a single brain (or perhaps a handful of brains) to do its thinking. The resident enemy was relying on hundreds of active, engaged, and empowered brains to do its thinking. Success was up to the individual fighting man or woman.

General Clark changed the training. Instead of just concentrating on the skills of commanders, Clark focused on the frontline soldier. By training the frontline soldiers from the incoming battalions to think

---

29 W.K. Clark. A Time to Lead. Palgrave MacMillan, New York, NY, 2007 p. 136

on their feet, they were able to change battle outcomes. Corp discipline engaged the forces. Individual, on-the-spot ingenuity determined its outcome. The commander's job was to enable the frontline soldier. Fundamental to a successful military squad is mutual trust, full personal engagement, and empowerment to accomplish the mission at hand. Trust, Engage, Empower.

The level of trust, engagement, and empowerment in a company's workforce rests fully on the shoulders of the commander. In any business, it rests on the shoulders of the CEO.

Harry Davis, professor at the University of Chicago's Booth School of Business, talks about the four Ps of innovation. His fourth P is the CEO's personal philosophy of leadership. Davis admits that while it is the fourth P, it is really the foundation.[30] Without a personal philosophy of leadership that seeks to actualize each individual's potential, the CEO lacks the foundation of great leadership.

The good news is that we all choose our personal philosophy. If, tomorrow, you want to have the personal philosophy of a leader, you can. Likewise, anyone can learn to be a great leader. It just takes passion, know-how, and practice.

The first step to turning a company into an innovation powerhouse is a little bit like stepping off a cliff. The company will abandon practices that inhibit workers' ability to innovate. Most of these

---

30 Harry Davis: Roger L. and Rachel M. Goetz Distinguished Service Professor of Creative Management, at University of Chicago in a talk titled "Leading Innovative Organizations," given January 6, 2009 at the Innovation Roundtable in the Gleacher Center, at the University of Chicago.

practices will be supported by the rigid mindset that believes these practices are necessary and correct.

Truisms

The *old normal* manager believes:

- We can't do everything.
- We can only afford so many development projects.
- Our current share of market is good.
- There are only so many good people.
- There will always be projects on our cut-off list.
- We've got to make a healthy profit first.

(The person who created the list labeled it "the old conventional thinking." For him it is a roadmap to failure. Whose list is it? It's Robert Galvin's list. During his tenure, Motorola manufactured and sold world-changing technologies, like the first color televisions, the first cellular telephones, and space communications, including transmitting the words "one small step for man, one giant leap for mankind." Not only did his leadership take Motorola through technological change, but his company was one of the first to respond successfully to competition from the Japanese. They were sure-footed in all their moves at the time.)

Does it sound like a reasonable list of truisms? Statements like, "we can't do everything" and "we can only afford so many development projects" sound fine. But they are roadblock statements. These statements are designed to feel comfortable because they don't present a problem; rather, they present a state of being. Posing a problem might be "why can't we do everything?" or better yet, "how can we do everything?"

But if we stick with, "we can't do everything," for the moment, what do we mean by *everything*? Is the meaning something like, "we have a lot of good ideas, but there's just no way we can pursue all of them." What about the "crazy" ideas? Well, if we can't pursue all the good ideas, we certainly won't pursue any crazy ideas! We've already talked about the best ideas. They sound crazy at first. If you forgo the crazy ideas, then you'll forgo the best ideas. If you forgo the best ideas, you will eventually lose your competitive advantage.

Or might "we can't do everything" mean that we cannot play in every niche of our customer base? This notion says that, ultimately, we will give something up to the competition because the customer subgroup is just not mainstream enough. However, every breakthrough starts out as a niche product. Either you own the customer relationship, or some competitor will.

If, as CEO, you are struggling inside with the idea of tossing out this list, you are not alone. Most of your competitors feel the same way. It is a common mindset. But, like many "conventional" things, it is where the opportunity hides.

One Step at a Time

The CEO needs to overcome this mindset in all layers of management. In some respects, this is the single most difficult challenge. Fortunately, the individual steps are small.

The CEO will lead by being out front, and to do that, he first needs to answer the question, what really matters to me? CEOs who believe that the best way to manage is through a highly structured decision hierarchy where meaningful decisions are made only at the top, who think "we can't do everything," who don't currently see anyone in the organization ready to take on the CEO role, and are concerned with how they stack up against other CEOs in terms of compensation, etc., are probably not well positioned to produce the most long-term value for the company. The board of directors should be looking for some sort of change.

The CEO who focuses on creating competitive advantage will recognize that in the new normal you have to be better than the competition at problem solving. The company will need its entire workforce to be engaged in problem solving. To engage that workforce, the first necessary condition is to establish trust and to empower the staff. Knowing how to do this is crucial.

Where a CEO seeks to transform his or her company into the competitive powerhouse in its industry, then engagement is what matters. As CEO, you want people to be engaged in solving problems and building competitive advantage *for the company*. One way or another, people are engaged all the time. The problem most companies face is that employees are engaged in something other than solving problems for the company.

If personal safety and security are in doubt, then people will be focused on becoming safe and secure. Personal safety and security in the workplace amount to worries about job-security and advancement. These worries are ever-present factors, which can take priority over the other engagers.

Unfortunately, the behaviors of many managers raise their subordinates' concerns over safety and security. Often, safety and security remain constant concerns and will dominate the employees' engagement. In this circumstance, the first priority will always be safety and security; everything else can be sacrificed in the face of that, including truth and the interests of the company. This was part of Roger Smith's failure at GM. His treatment of employees undermined their sense of security.

You cannot get engagement without building trust and empowering employees to use their talents.

Knowing how to instill trust, engagement, and empowerment is the finger in the calf's mouth. These are things not taught in business school. G.OL.F. T.E.E.™ is a set of best practices that create the culture of innovation. They are all tried and true techniques. You start by understanding why the framework must address certain fundamental human issues.

TRUST

Trust is a foundational element to establishing and maintaining an innovative culture. People produce bold ideas where truth trumps trepidation. Without trust, ideas are colored by their acceptability. Most people are just reluctant to take a risk on behalf of the company if they feel the risk of failure falls on them. Everyone in the company has to trust one another to deal honestly and openly with issues and opportunities.

Innovation is about problem solving, and good problem solving doesn't happen if the problem is not well understood. If the truth cannot be heard, then problems will not be well understood. As you rise in the hierarchy, you are more distant from the truth.

When Nell Minow became president of Institutional Shareholder Services, her predecessor, Bob Monks gave her this succinct insight: "Watch how funny your jokes get."

Nell says, "I need to remind myself constantly of the challenge that gets tougher and tougher as you get higher in the organization to get people to be honest with you."[31]

Truth depends on trust.

The CEO plays two critical roles in creating trust. First, the CEO establishes how the company will deal with the risks and rewards associated with innovative initiatives. Second, the CEO establishes the environment for interactions between and among all the people in the company—this is what culture is. The goal is to establish an environment where all the relationships are on an adult-to-adult level and everyone is engaged in his or her work. Truth is the only good basis for decision making, and you want to be sure everyone is free to push forward the truth. Motorola's famous former CEO Robert Galvin tenaciously pursued truth. One day after a meeting, a young engineer approached him: "Bob, I heard that point you made this morning, and I think you are dead wrong. I'm going to prove it. I'm going to shoot you down." Reportedly, Galvin proudly turned to his companion and said, "That's how we've overcome Texas Instruments' lead in semiconductors!"[32] He understood that the company was better off if everyone felt comfortable being candid with the CEO.

The T in TEE is trust. We said earlier that if the truth cannot be heard, then problems will not be well understood. It doesn't hurt to have an explicit company policy: "*In this company we tell the truth,*

---

31   Adam Bryant, Think 'We' for Best Results, , New York Times, accessed 11/13/2009 http://www.nytimes.com/2009/04/19/business/19corner.html?pagewanted =1&sq=Nell%20Minow&st=cse&adxnnl=1&scp=3&adxnnlx=1240323287-3K7mpnEMI6rkMMvgHEdsRw
32   Maria Leopoldina posted 14 July 2008, wordreference.com, accessed 11/13/2009, http://forum.wordreference.com/showthread.php?t=1031815

even when the truth is hard to take. "When people are not truthful in a company, it is because they feel personal risk in telling the truth. Nell Minow commented about management styles in poorly performing companies:

> All of them had CEOs who took an enormous number of steps to make sure that no one would ever question them or second-guess them. At one of the companies we were involved in, we talked to a number of employees who all used the same phrase—if you disagree with the boss, you get fired on the spot.

A CEO would be foolish to put himself or herself in the position where he or she is identified with some specific idea. A wise CEO knows how to get others to take ownership of good ideas. This leaves the CEO a good way to back-out if he or she subsequently gets more and better information, which negates the value of the original idea. Fear gets in the way of truth telling. The antidote to fear is trust.

Ambiguity and Uncertainty Avoidance

Geert Hofstede has done considerable work around human differences and how they define cultures. The four principal differences he looks at are:[33]

---

33 If you want more information about Hofstede's work, go to http://www.geert-hofstede.com/geert_hofstede_resources.shtml or to his personal Web site http://feweb.uvt.nl/center/hofstede/index.htm.

- Power Distance Index (PDI)
- Individualism (IDV)
- Masculinity/Femininity (MAS)
- Uncertainty Avoidance Index (UAI)

Power Distance Index is how the less powerful in a group accept an unequal distribution of power; Individualism is a measure of how important to the culture the ties are among individuals; Masculinity/Femininity is about the nature of roles between the genders and the difference in their values; and Uncertainty Avoidance Index deals with a culture's ability to cope with ambiguity and risk.

In preparation for a presentation at a university in the Chicago area, I compared Hofstede's indexes for individual countries to their level of innovation as indicated by their per capita patent activity. It turns out the first three have no strong correlation to innovation, but Uncertainty Avoidance Index is strongly correlated to how innovative the culture is. According to Dr. Hofstede, this index ultimately refers to a culture's approach to man's search for truth.

In innovative organizations, the culture is tolerant of opinions different from the current doctrine. Organizations innovate when they have as few rules as possible, and the rules that do exist are made to be broken.

The opposite culture that already "knows the truth" has set it in stone. It will have lots and lots of rules, one of which is that individuals have no need to keep looking for truth. People in this culture have a high Uncertainty Avoidance Index.

As individual humans, each of us has a limited capacity to deal with ambiguity. The greater the ambiguity affects the individual, the more he will focus on removing it. That is, if a person feels great ambiguity about when and where his next meal is coming from, he will be focused on removing that ambiguity.

Likewise in the workplace, the more ambiguity around factors that affect the individual's survival and success, the more the individual will focus efforts on removing the ambiguity. Earlier, we pointed out that companies that use forced ranking find it impossible to create simple measurable goals. The reason for this is simple. Most people are honest and hard working. If you establish clear, achievable stretch goals, most people will beat them. If you then have to put them into a ranking, you are faced with problems. Some of them are going to have to go into the bottom third.

The way companies deal with this problem is to include some subjective criteria. These subjective criteria give managers a lever to adjust performance evaluation to fit the curve. But this creates a level of ambiguity because everyone knows the manager has to fit people into a curve and that bias (favoritism) will play a role. This creates an element of risk for every person in a subordinate role and colors the dialogue. Truth suffers.

$ Innovative companies want their employees to focus on removing the ambiguity associated with customer problems. To the extent that unrelated but preoccupying ambiguities can be removed, the ability of employees to focus on the customer increases. A good way to deal with this is to create an Antiambiguity Team to identify these preoccupying ambiguities and develop ways to eliminate them.

Who's Risk Is It?

Effective innovation companies have great problem solvers. In any company, these people are typically not very good at navigating the politics of internal influence. They get it wrong so much of the time that they try to avoid it, which makes an ambiguous corporate management system particularly difficult for them. A necessary condition for effectively surmounting this is to be absolutely clear on how the company deals with risk.

A key to effective risk management is to distinguish between an anticipated risk and an unexpected risk. The anticipated risk is easier to deal with, but an unexpected risk can sometimes be so serious that it dominates management attention. Often, this risk has nothing to do with innovation per se, but its high-pressure nature reveals the company's true response to risk. It is in these circumstances that employees see whether or not executives walk the talk.

Situations like this can bring out the worst in people—or the best. When a medical devices company was just about to go for final FDA approval on an important new sterile device, they were surprised to discover a high level of microbial contamination on the final product. Since the device's intended use was in surgery, this contamination was a showstopper. A significant investment, along with market opportunity, would be lost; the future of the company was at stake. The problem got everyone's attention, but because the materials for the device came from various suppliers, the cause of contamination wasn't clear. It created an opportunity for lots of finger pointing. In this case, management prevented that from happening.

Part of the CEO's role is to be especially alert when the pressure is on and ensure finger pointing never gets started. Blame serves no constructive purpose. Find the problem, fix it, learn from it, and move on. If you want an innovative company, you must have a safe environment for taking risks. The best rule of thumb is to avoid blame entirely, even when the action is blameworthy. If someone is going to be fired, make it clear that taking a risk didn't cause the problem; it was caused by an employee's deliberate act to hurt the company.

In the case of the medical devices team, the problem arose during the shipping and handling of a large component. It became highly charged with static electricity, which attracted millions of particles of contamination from within the environment. The fix was a simple change in handling and the inclusion of de-ionizing equipment.

Planned innovation involves risk too. Whether the innovation is delivered as a result of some individual effort or through a team effort, the company should have a mandatory methodology in place for identifying and estimating the risk associated with the innovation initiative. The point is to be able to mitigate the risks as much as possible and as early as possible and monitor the development of risk as the innovation project proceeds. It is important to establish an approach that encourages and enables innovators to identify risks. (When we talk about tools, we will talk about something we call a flexible risk-gate process to reduce risk in the most cost-effective manner.) But there are times when even an obvious risk (in hindsight) is not identified before it creates damage. The point of identifying risks is to mitigate them where possible. A risk-gate process vets the risks in a formal manner. Whether or not an innovator or her team identifies all the risks is not a criterion of performance.

$ For innovation to take place throughout the company, people need to know what's at stake for them personally. The best ways to deal with this is to ensure that once a project gets a go-ahead, the **risk becomes everyone's risk**. This should be an explicit company policy. Innovation involves risk, and sometimes the risks manifest losses. Failure goes with the territory, and risk takers should never have to fear punishment. The only things you should correct are inaction, negligence, and sabotage.

Truth Among Adults

For it to be a truthful conversation, the parties must trust one another. In this they are equal. They each must trust that the other seeks truth first, above everything else.

Trust is a two-way relationship.

> You cannot establish trust if you cannot listen. A conversation is a relationship. Both speaker and listener play a part, each influencing the other. Instead of being a passive recipient, the listener has as much to do in shaping the conversation as the speaker.[34]

In talking with a colleague who'd had the opportunity to work with Roger Smith of GM, this colleague complained that Roger did not listen. Listening wasn't Roger's only shortcoming, but it was a debilitating handicap. If you think you have all the answers, then listening is hard to do.

A friend of mine worked as the innovation guru at a large insurance company. The CEO had a product idea and a year before had two senior VPs work on developing the product. After an initial investigative period, the two SVPs realized that the idea was a nonstarter; it was not wanted in the market. Knowing the CEO would not like this news, they each "found" that they could no longer devote the time to the project it required because their normal day-to-day responsibilities were too demanding. The project was then placed on the shoulders of my friend. The CEO insisted that he develop the product and put it into production. A year and a half and nearly $5 million later, the product failed in the marketplace. My friend took the hit and lost his job.

$ Great leaders know that no matter how brilliant they think their own ideas are, chances are that someone else will be able to improve on them. Listening is the first necessary and essential ability

---

34 *Selling With NLP*, Kerry L. Johnson

to getting to the right problem and the right solution. Listening is foundational to sustaining competitive advantage.

In Western culture, we place the responsibility for the meaning of the conversation on the speaker. However, in some Eastern cultures, the responsibility rests with the listener. It is an interesting point of view. Communication isn't just about the speaker—both parties must take responsibility. The end result is mutual understanding.

Typically, when adults interact, they interact on an adult-to-adult basis. However, in many company structures, when a subordinate interacts with a superior, the relationship ceases to be adult-to-adult. The hierarchical structure imposes an adult-to-child relationship. This is not always obvious to an outside observer. The two people can appear to be interacting as adults, but the dialogue contains clues to the true nature of the relationship. Benjamin Disraeli was once asked how he managed to get so much favor from the queen. "I never deny, I never contradict, and I sometimes forget." In other words, he conducts himself in a subservient way to gain favor, and truth is allowed to suffer.

In hierarchical structures, the superior is talking down to the subordinate, and the subordinate is responding in ways that will generate the least negative consequence. The subordinate is trying to please the superior, just as a child tries to please an adult. The easiest way to determine if this is taking place is to look at the superior's words. If the same words could have been said in the same way by the subordinate, then they are on an adult-to-adult level. If not, then they are interacting on an adult-to-child level.

"I am not interested in what you think. Just do as you're told." You can certainly imagine a superior saying that to a subordinate. The same could be said of the following:

> Did I not make this clear to you?
> Are you lazy or just incompetent?
> Did you not understand the assignment?
> You should have thought of that first, don't you think?
> Do I have to do everything myself to get it done right?
> What in the world were you thinking?

Usually the adult-to-child talk is subtler, sometimes it is just the tone of what is said, but the effect is the same. When a superior uses sarcastic, condescending, rude, or hateful language, the subordinate cannot respond in kind. The relationship is adult-to-child, and truth will suffer in that environment.

Ensuring a truthful environment depends on keeping the conversation at an adult-to-adult level. The easiest way to ensure this exists is to establish a one-sentence people-management manual. It is the golden rule of management:

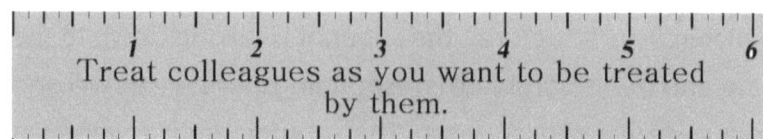

Treat colleagues as you want to be treated by them. This implies that a person in a leadership role can reasonably understand how he or she would feel on the receiving end of the action. Treat colleagues as you want to be treated by them is a simple rule to establish and a wonderful way to ensure leadership prevails over management. The flip side for the nonleadership employees is to Treat your leaders with the same level of respect they show you. It will keep your leaders honest. [35]

It helps to keep in mind that stockholders are not interested in the personal empires being built by middle and senior managers. Moreover, enlightened stockholders are against empire building, because it undermines trust, engagement, and empowerment. The board of directors has oversight responsibility to make sure the hierarchy is about leadership, resource allocation, and strategy development, and to ensure it is <u>not</u> about power and prestige.

A couple of other things that can act as fulcrum points to ensure an organization moves toward adult-to-adult relationships are:

First, change all internal job titles to something along the lines of *colleague*. At W.L. Gore & Associates everyone is an *associate*. Instead of bosses, they have *sponsors*.[36]

$ In this model, everyone has the job title like *colleague*. Some colleagues have an additional role as *team leader*. But the team leader title is only used by members of that team. The only person who is team leader to everyone is the CEO. All other team leaders are just colleague to most people in the company.

---

35   A recent management book I ran across said that this golden rule idea is nonsense. And it is true, but only if you think what makes a company a good competitor is an autocratic visionary leader like Roger Smith. But I think the authors of that book were mistaken.
36   If you want good insight into an innovative culture, page through Gore's Web site: http://www.gore.com/en_xx/aboutus/culture/index.html.

Truth is more likely to be spoken where everyone interacts as colleagues. This seems like a small insignificant change, but that is what a fulcrum point is—the point where a small change fosters a gradual mutation of the environment that in hindsight looks big. If *colleague* isn't a comfortable word for your company, use a synonym like associate, fellow, cast member, crew member, coworker, collaborator, compatriot, comrade, partner, team mate, or work mate. You could also use a derivative of the company name, e.g., IBMer, Googlite, Southwesterner, Citigrouper, or Amazonian.

Second, go through the employee handbook and policy manual, and remove all language that describes relationships in terms of power and position, e.g., senior, junior, superior, or subordinate. Eliminate paragraphs that talk about managing within this hierarchical structure. It will be easy to find volunteers within the company to help with this project.

Truth helps deal with risk. People within a company are very adept when it comes to sniffing out disingenuous statements. National Public Radio reported once on a GM program called the Product Evaluation Program. Every six months, the program distributes 8,000 vehicles to 8,000 employees and pays for most of the gasoline the employees put into the vehicles. The company says it's an important tool: employees must make routine reports to an internal Web site and immediately identify problems. Ostensibly, this is a quality control program.

At this level it looks reasonable, but dig a little deeper and you realize that of the 240,000 employees working for GM, most are blue collar workers. GM makes vehicles targeted at the blue collar worker. You could reasonably expect that GM would take advantage of this fit and distribute blue collar vehicles to blue collar workers, and to really get valuable input from these people, GM would distribute the 8,000 vehicles to a different set of 8,000 people every six months. However, blue collar workers don't participate in the program, which is a perk for white collar employees. The vehicles go to the same set of white collar employees every six months.

💲 Perks are a problem when it comes to engagement, but here the issue is truth. GM is dressing up a perk in clothes of a different color. If it described the program as a quality program of sorts and a perk for certain employees, then at least truth would be served. By pretending it is just a quality program, it is being disingenuous and that undermines trust.

Truth is much harder than you think.

Actually it is *what you think* as leader that makes truth so hard. It is what all of us think that gets in the way of seeing truth. Each of us carry around a basketful of biases. For the most part, we are unaware that we have these biases.

We live within our own dogmas, and like pre-Einstein physicists, we firmly believe a whole set of *proven* ideas that someday will turn out to be wrong. The bottom line is that the best ideas we will encounter in our lives will sound wrong at first. We are at most risk of missing the truth in that moment of most certainty.

Great advances in human knowledge always had to overcome the then current thinking to become the new current thinking.

 In business, the wise CEO, who "knows" the idea is wrong, will come up with a way to test this knowledge with the least cost. That is because the wise CEO knows history: in business, frequently the best ideas must overcome the CEO's objections to them.

Much of the discussion below on engagement and empowerment is about establishing methods to allow the CEO to be wrong at first and right in maximizing stockholder value.

ENGAGE

"The beatings will cease when morale improves."—Pirate T-Shirt

Everybody in your company comes to work and engages in activities that create meaning for their lives. The CEO cannot (nor should he or she want to) change that fundamental fact, i.e., workplace activities impact how employees define their sense of self-worth. How individual employees deal with this fundamental truth will determine the long-term level of prosperity of the firm. Lately good books like *Making Meaning* by Diller, Shedroff, and Rhea instruct businesses to create products and services that deliver meaning to customers. This is the right message. However, the ability to create meaning for customers in a sustained and competitive way first depends on the CEO's ability to align the individual employees work with a profound sense of their self worth. First create meaning for employees, then for customers. This is what engagement is all about.

NUMMI

We started this book with the story of Roger Smith who was both an industry visionary, and a lousy CEO. He failed to engage his employees. So it is ironic that perhaps the best example of a truly innovative company is the Fremont, California, automobile assembly plant called NUMMI, which was right under Roger's nose. It is a story about the value of people and the results of good leadership. Anyone who wants to build an innovative company should read the story of this plant. It is a testament to the value of aligning work to people's sense of self-worth. You can easily find the NUMMI story on the Web.[37] Since I suspect many of you already know the story, I will only hit the relevant highlights here.

---

37 http://www.ob.shudo-u.ac.jp/jimuhp/souken/web/magazine/pdf/com/shou47-2austenfeld.pdf

In 1982, the General Motors plant in Fremont, California, was operating significantly below par in terms of cost and quality. In fact, it was GM's poorest performing plant on both measures. In addition, the plant was plagued with very contentious labor problems. On any given day, as many as 20 percent of the workforce failed to show up for work, and sometimes on Mondays and Fridays there were too few workers to start the assembly line. Evident also, was a significant drug and alcohol abuse problem. The plant management had to hire a special clean-up crew to clear the parking lots of drug and alcohol paraphernalia after shift changes. Due to threats of violence from workers, some supervisors came to work armed with mace. Additionally, the unionized workforce had more than 5,000 unanswered grievances on file. Recognizing the product produced was lousy, and the workforce was unredeemable, General Motors closed the plant and laid off the entire workforce.

Around the same time, Toyota, which had enjoyed growing market share in the United States, wanted to preserve that rich market opportunity. With a serious recession looming, the Japanese company was concerned that the U.S. government, under pressure to preserve U.S. jobs, would impose overt (and subtle technical) import restrictions. Toyota felt their best strategy would be to begin assembling cars in the United States, and since it lacked experience in the U.S. labor market, it looked for an industry partner that could smooth the transition. Toyota began joint venture discussions with GM, and when an agreement was reached, the Fremont plant fit the bill. It was relatively new, properly equipped, and, most importantly, it was available. General Motors, which was very interested in learning the Japanese production methods, disclosed the labor problems to Toyota, but Toyota felt it could deal with the issues.

Toyota hired 85 percent of the workforce GM had laid off. Everyone went through training in the Toyota methods of running an automobile manufacturing facility, which included sending over 400 team and group leaders to Japan for hands-on experience. When the plant reopened in 1985, the workers had a single pay grade, a single job description, with the job title *team member*. (GM had over eighty different job descriptions, each with variable pay.) Toyota organized the work around a small team of five to seven workers who rotated stations on the line every couple of hours. The Toyota plant had just three levels of management: team leaders (a union member), group leaders, and plant management. Toyota also instituted a no-layoff policy.

The key to the success of this plant was the sense of self-worth each worker shared as a team member to continually look for and implement ways to do things better. This culture of innovation wasn't a management mandate. It came naturally to the workforce because of Toyota's practice of asking five *why* questions to get to the important answer. The question is "Why is what you do important?" For example, imagine a tax collector answering the question.

> "Because if I didn't do this, people wouldn't pay their taxes."
> "Why is that important?"
> "Because the government needs the money."
> "Why is that important?"
> "Because without money, the government couldn't fund schools, build roads, provide emergency services, etc."
> "Why is that important?"

"Because those things make people's lives better."

"Ah! I see. You collect taxes to improve people's lives!"

Using this simple technique, Toyota ties every individual's work to the goal of making the world a better place (or something equivalent). Then to make that a real engine of excellence and innovation, it did what any company can do. It put people together in small teams with the worthy goal of making the world better as their bond. People on that kind of mission need no management. They may occasionally need support or resources, but they don't need to be told to build a quality product or to find ways to do things better. They do those things naturally because that is behavior consistent with their personal values.

During the first full year of production starting in 1985, 90 percent of team members contributed innovative ideas, and more than 10,000 of these were implemented. This was not a fluke—innovation continued at this pace every year. For example, thirteen years into operation of the plant, 86 percent of team members made at least one suggestion, at a rate of 3.2 ideas per worker, with 81 percent of the innovations being implemented.

Toyota did not hire everyone. They were very thorough in their hiring practice and wasted no time in releasing people who were ill suited for the environment. Where GM saw unredeemable employees, Toyota found perfectly capable people. This is one of the most remarkable statements of the value of people, and it is an even greater statement of the value of leadership. It also highlights the fact that people come up to (or down to) the level management sets for them. Moreover, Toyota showed that virtually everyone can be an innovative problem solver. Any company should ask "Does our environment allow people to invent and implement these solutions?"

$ Linking the employee's personal values to the work he or she performs creates engagement. The closer you can link a person's performance to the person's definition of self, the more engaged the person will be. Engagement is the personal motivator for every employee. Unfortunately, many companies lack good leadership, and as a consequence, the day the employee is most engaged is his or her first day on the job. From that point forward, engagement erodes until the employee is no longer engaged. One study suggests that normally about 16 percent of all employees are actively disengaged.

One NUMMI team member said that the new system gave him pride in his work, a sense of belonging to something bigger and more important, and almost everyone could point to some change they'd come up with that improved the product or process. That kind of engagement is valuable because it is correlated to higher levels of individual performance, and it is the only sustainable motivator—far more powerful than money.

When it comes to money as a motivator, an often pointed to exception is a salesperson. However, we ran into an insurance broker who was dismayed that most of his sales team, who were over fifty-years-old, had stopped being aggressive producers. They'd built their book sufficiently to live with a bigger income than they'd ever expected to have and now needed only to maintain the book. When money is the sole motivator, *enough* undermines the need to keep selling. Money was undermining sales motivation in this case. The only way to turn this around was to link something of greater value than money to the sales effort.

$ Toyota knows how to do this. The spectacular turnaround of the workforce at NUMMI had nothing to do with paying employees more. Everyone on the line had the same salary and job. Toyota understood that the individual worker's internal values, shared across a team, are what generate the self-motivation needed for problem-solving and productive behaviors.

Muhammad Yunus, who shared the 2006 Nobel Peace Prize,[38] understood this idea of linking personal values to the work performed. His Grameen bank established a set of stars signifying achievement of a particular goal for a branch. If the branch achieved all five goals, the branch received all five stars. The staff pursued these stars with a passion, even though the bank attached no financial incentives to the achievement. In his book *Banker to the Poor*, Yunus wrote, "They are not doing it for any monetary benefit. They are doing it...to prove their worth to themselves."

Yunus understood that people come up to, or down to, the level set for them by their environment. He wrote, "One cannot but wonder how an environment can make people despair and sit idle and then, by changing the conditions, one can transform the same people into matchless performers." He saw this remarkable aspect of the human condition, just as Toyota had seen it. People respond to the environment into which they are thrust. To let them be their best, leaders need to establish the right environment to allow people the opportunity to prove their worth to themselves.

---

38 In 2006, the Nobel Peace prize was split evenly between Muhammad Yunus and his Grameen Bank for their efforts to create economic and social development from below.

Creating policies that nurture engagement is crucial. When Toyota opened the NUMMI plant, they established a no layoff policy. The policy simply stated that layoffs would be the last resort, and spelled out other tactics including salary cuts (deepest at the top) that would be used first. The message of engagement resonated with the workforce since they'd all suffered unemployment as a result of the GM layoff.

Similarly, when Jürgen Dormann took over ABB with its 180,000 employees, he had an enormous crisis. The company faced huge debt, a worsening economy, spiraling costs, bad management, and asbestos-related litigation. He felt a responsibility to everyone affected—employees and their families. He wrote to every employee and explained how dire the situation was but that layoffs would be the last, worst option. The people in the company engaged in the quest for ways to cut costs and save the company. Over the next two years, the team found ways to save $1 billion. Dormann had created a policy that engaged the workforce.

Libby Sartain, who at one time ran HR for Southwest Airlines, points out that the biggest contributor to layoffs is the way people are hired in good times. Many companies pursue aggressive hiring activities in good times in the mistaken belief that they must hire the best talent or else the competition will get them. This is a glass-half-empty view of the world. These companies expand their workforce beyond levels of need, and when the economy hits a bump in the road, they suddenly find themselves with overly fat payrolls.

Jürgen Dormann and the leadership at Toyota realize that the best people are the people they already have. The installed workforce is rich with valuable tacit knowledge about the company and its products. If you engage these people, they will be extraordinarily innovative and hard working. Libby Sartain suggests the only way to hire is to hire knowing that sooner or later the economy will hit a rough spot.

Perks

Perks, which are general in nature, usually make rational sense and do not create a problem for engagement. They are not really perquisites in the sense that they are not really about privilege. Take the company with a policy that all employees fly coach, except when traveling overseas and then they fly business class. The reason for this difference is because employees have a better chance of sleeping on the plane in business class. After a long flight, they will arrive at their destination better prepared to work. It is a policy that applies to all employees.

This kind of policy can evolve into a perk. One of the world's major credit card brands entered into a contract with a major airline for a discount as long an employees chose that airline over the competition. As a consequence, the airline gave the company a number of upgrade certificates. But, there were not enough certificates to go around. Instead of handing them out on a first-come-first-served basis, the company held on to them, only giving them out to senior executives when they traveled. This is privilege. It was supposed to be a secret policy, but it is ridiculous to think that would be kept quiet, and, of course, it wasn't.

Perks that apply to a subset of employees imply privilege. The employees who don't enjoy the perks see themselves as second class, undervalued employees, and employees who do get them develop a sense of entitlement. Perks that apply to only certain employees undermine engagement every time. Companies with the most engaged workforce ensure that each individual employee is highly and equally valued.

It is doubly unfortunate when companies use the hierarchy as a basis for distributing different levels of perks. The higher you go in the company, the more perks you enjoy. This means that everyone in the company, other than the top dog, is undervalued because there is some level of perks they don't enjoy, and it seems unfair.

$ When Dormann joined ABB, he surprised his executive team when he boarded a flight and walked past them in first class to sit in coach. He believes the CEO must model humility at all times.

Trust, Engagement, and Empowerment (TEE) are all linked together. In the case of engagement, studies of employee engagement suggest that the single most critical driver of high engagement is the ability of employees to use their talents. Empowerment is what enables employees to use their talents. Empowerment is critical to both engagement and to the company's capability to solve problems.

Empowerment

In *Weird Ideas That Work*, Robert Sutton tells of a time when an executive from a large manufacturing corporation was pressuring him "to give him a step-by-step recipe, the precise details, the exact schedule, for transforming his organization into one that is routinely innovative…My answer was…'hire a bunch of smart people and stay out of the way until they ask for help.'"

Empowerment is about giving employees the ability to deliver against their ideas. Empowered employees are authorized and enabled to do what they determine is needed to deliver against goals. In the case of NUMMI, the role of group leader was focused on providing employees with the resources needed to take their ideas to the next step. It could be engineering help, it could be supplies, or it could be a design team.

Explicit empowerment can set the stage. At Gore "teams organize around opportunities and leaders emerge." We've seen that 3M pioneered the idea of giving employees the ability to set aside time to work on special projects. Google gives its engineers *20 percent time*, so that they're free to work on what they're really passionate about. Google's belief in empowerment can be summed up as, "give the proper tools to a group of people who like to make a difference, and they will."[39]

Recently, one of my partners and I attended a program on product innovation at one of the excellent universities in the Chicago area. The speaker was a professor at the university and CEO of a firm, which specializes in product development. He spent the second half of the program going through a complex, rigid stage-gate process. My partner looked over at me and frowned. I knew exactly what he was thinking.

Stage-gate processes are about reducing risk, but they can kill innovation. There is a large mobile phone manufacturer in the area that currently employs a rigid stage-gate process. In a conversation with one of its engineers, he told me about a cool idea a colleague of his came up with. The trouble was the idea was far enough removed from the mobile phone model that the stage-gate process did not fit. The process killed the idea in the early stage.

A key to allowing people to pursue ideas is to establish a flexible Risk-gate™ process. This process facilitates the least expensive, but

---

39 Google corporate site, "Our Philosophy", Accessed 11/14/2009 http://www.google.com/corporate/tenthings.html

best use of resources to pass an idea through a primary risk. The basic purpose of the flexible Risk-gate™ process is to vet the idea in terms of what knowledge is missing.[40] Select the next easiest, cheapest, but meaningful risk to resolve and come up with a strategy to remove that risk. Such risks could be about what form factor a product should have, will customers accept the product,—perhaps a prototype is needed. Or perhaps a manufacturing step is needed that's never been done before—find a way to test the step or develop alternatives. Or perhaps you don't know if the technology will work when it's put together with other parts—test building a working model.

$ One blanket way to minimize early stage risk is the *20 percent time* solution. The 20 percent time is a way to allow early stage risks to be contained to this small package of an individual's time. It works well at Google because development work often can be pursued by an individual or a small cooperating team. W.L. Gore & Associates' approach allows ideas to bubble up until a team is needed to take it to the next level. As the need for additional resources increases, the team grows.

At 3M, the CEO who nearly killed the idea for masking tape recognized the limitations in his own ability to recognize a good idea and that an employee with a passion should be allowed to pursue an idea. This approach paid off in 1968, when Spencer Silver discovered his unique adhesive that Art Fry, later turned into Post-it® Notes.

It took eight years for the Post-it® Notes to reach the market. This story illustrates how much time may pass, from creating a solution,

---

40 Launchpad Partners has a robust product to enable companies to manage this process with confidence that the project is following the most efficient and effective early stage process.

to finding the right problem, to launching the product. The key lesson here is to find ways to avoid killing ideas without breaking the bank. The mobile phone manufacturer killed an idea early, but 3M didn't.

If Art Fry had to go through a stage-gate process for his hymnal bookmark, the process would have required a business plan containing business goals, a market analysis, financial analysis, technical evaluation, and competitive research. (These requirements are taken from the "front end" of an actual stage gate process.) You can almost hear someone kill the idea with, "Look, if there were any kind of market for hymnal bookmarks, someone would already be in that space. It's a nonstarter."

One approach to dealing with the issue, particularly in environments where it is difficult for a single employee to advance a solution alone, is to establish a flexible Risk-gate™ funding pool. Keep in mind that the purpose of a risk gate is to minimize risk. A flexible risk gate process enables you to establish project-specific milestones while remaining flexible about what those milestones are and who needs to be involved.

$ The employees involved identify what the next critical risk factor is and determine what they must overcome and which approach has the smallest possible investment. Some ideas need a couple of hundred dollars to move to the next stage, but others may need thousands. The mantra for all employees is to preserve cash and look for creative ways to move an idea along without creating an unnecessary financial risk.

One example:

To hedge the bet on any idea, establish a link between engagement and funding. In this method, substituting for some measurement of engagement is the number of employees signing on to the project.

No colleague can come to the pool alone; there must be at least two people. Two people can get up to $5,000, for example. But if the first risk only requires an investment of $378, then the two-person team still has remaining budget to work the next risk. Let the leftover money accumulate.

If even more money is needed, then a larger number of people must join the team. How you structure this depends on the funding need in the company, but it might look something like:

- *3 employees <= $10,000*
- *4 employees <= $20,000*
- *5 employees <= $50,000*

By allowing associates to sign on to no more than two teams in a six-month period, you build in a risk control governor. Employees will want to work on teams where they believe the idea has potential.

This methodology gives everyone the opportunity to move a project along through its early stages without having to go through the unnecessary hurdles found in state-gate processes. As I pointed out earlier, the biggest obstacle to innovation is *mindset*. By empowering any worker to take an idea forward, the mindset issue is minimized. The worker may only need to convince one other person to get funding to move to the next stage.

$ Along the same lines is something we call the CEO Passion Pool™. This is an alternate funding source controlled solely by the CEO. This provides a pathway to employees when they are unsuccessful in getting anyone else interested in their idea. Plus, sometimes an employee will have such a good idea that it should be held close to the vest for a while. Employees can approach the CEO for funding for their idea, and at her sole discretion, the CEO may provide the requested funds.

Each CEO will naturally create his or her own criteria for funding an idea from the CEO Passion Pool. The CEO must keep in mind that his or her own mindset could filter out the best ideas. History has repeatedly shown that senior management does a poor job of judging ideas. Since it is called the Passion Pool perhaps the best criterion is the level of passion the creator has for the idea. Normally it takes a good deal of personal commitment for anyone to approach the CEO. If the creator can articulate the problem and the solution then you at least have some notion of the potential for the idea. Perhaps a good reminder is that ideas like a hymnal bookmark hardly seem powerful or even worthwhile. Robert Galvin, the CEO of Motorola, back when the company was an innovation powerhouse, suggested that trusting a person's passions is an act of faith that "things are doable that are not necessarily provable." Galvin was a strong advocate of trust, engagement, and empowerment. Because the CEO can pull in needed resources, the idea can be vetted, not for its inherent value, but to determine the next, least-expensive, reasonable step. This keeps the idea alive but limits the investment risk to the minimal next step.

Additionally, a clever CEO can use an advisory core made up of independent supersynthesizers to evaluate the clarity of the problem definition and the fit of the solution. Supersynthesizers in this role can add great value in fine-tuning both the problem definition and the solution. It is important to employ a supersynthesizer who is not very familiar with the problem under discussion. Fresh perspective is essential, but more essential is that supersynthesis talent to see the big picture with ability to understand what details matter, and what details are missing or incomplete. Getting this level of problem definition right makes the process more effective and often more efficient because it allows you to sidestep some hidden issue that will otherwise surely arise in the future. Task the supersynthesizer to evaluate the problem and solution, not for the business value of the solution, but rather for the clarity of the problem definition and the fit of the solution to that definition. [41]

$ Both, the team funding method and the CEO passion pool benefit from a monitoring process. As ideas advance through a flexible risk-gate process, the people involved begin to develop mindsets. Sometimes, these mindsets can limit their ability to see alternative paths to pursue and the project runs out of gas. The role of the company leadership is to make sure that, when a project hits the doldrums, a fresh mind is employed to explore where the project is and how to keep it moving forward. This is a great role for a two-person team made up of a good leader and a supersynthesizer.

---

41   Our company has a tool to help people demonstrate their synthesis talent.

Problem/Solution Databases

$ When a business first creates internal tools like an idea warehouse or problem and solution databases, the expectation is that people inside the company will actively use it. The implementers believe people will come to the database to look up problems and solutions and contribute to ideas. Usually, it does not turn out that way. It gets a little use early on, and then withers on the vine.

But that's not always the case. There is a wonderful counter example from a company in Portugal called Sonaecom, which implemented its idea database with an innovative additional feature. It includes a game. The game operates like a stock market with ideas as the investment instruments. Each employee starts with a five thousand marketplace credits. These credits can be anonymously invested in various ideas people have put into the database. Employees can buy and sell ideas, always looking for the best ideas in which to invest. At the end of each month, employees can cash in their credits for various prizes ranging from fully paid-for vacations to mobile phones to merchandise. Of course to get the better prizes you need more credits. You need to propose good ideas or to make good idea investments.

Not everybody makes such good choices, as the COO of the company, Luis Filipe Reis, discovered. His choices did poorly in the marketplace, losing most of his credits. His experience underlines the discussion earlier that senior managers often are good at running organizations but not as good at recognizing great ideas from mediocre ones. For this, their role should be to empower and then trust the organization to make such distinctions. In Sonaecom's case this is done by, among others, recognizing the importance of their idea database for the company.

Even without such innovative additional features like Sonaecom's marketplace, the idea warehouse serves important purposes:

- Most importantly, it provides a mechanism to avoid killing an idea.
- Second, it provides a mechanism to allow the employee to move off one idea and work on something new. This is very important. Think about the story of the yarn breaking in the fabric factory. The employee with the solution held onto it for thirty-two years, but he didn't have anywhere to put the stake in the ground. It is fairly likely that he was stuck on that idea simply because he had no way to store it in a sanctioned way and move on to the next problem.
- Third, it provides a way to keep an idea percolating while the creator tries to build support for funding. Anyone can contribute memos to the database that will contribute to the thinking around the problem and solution.
- Fourth, it gives people across the company, who would not otherwise come into contact, a way to come together over a common problem.
- Fifth, it should be used to house competitor ideas around problem definition and solutions. Someone in senior management should be watching this part of the database looking for early warning signs that change is underway in the marketplace.

Innovation can start with either a problem or a solution. Thus, the problem database can house a defined problem for which no solution has yet been found. Likewise, the solution database can house a solution for an unidentified problem.

When a creator wants to move forward with funding for a project, there must be a problem in the problem database and a corresponding solution in the solution database and the two (or more) records must be linked. It is possible that a single solution solves more than one problem, just as a problem can have more than one solution. The solution database should also house the key risks that need to be addressed through the team's efforts. Additionally, the solution database must contain information describing who is on the project, when they joined, where supporting information can be obtained, and other information helpful in managing the activity around the solution.[42]

A Word About Passion

One day, a customer rolled a set of well-worn tires into his local Nordstrom store and demanded a refund. The clerk looked at the man and said, "Sir, how much did you pay for these tires?" The customer told him, and the clerk promptly refunded the exact amount and took the tires into the back room.

---

42 The author can provide a data definition model for both the Problem Database and the Solution Database, which lays out the structure and use of the tool.

This story is only remarkable from a customer-service perspective—not because the tires showed obvious signs of heavy use but because Nordstrom doesn't sell tires.

This is a business legend. Whether or not it's true, it's often repeated to illustrate Nordstrom's commitment to customer service. Nordstrom worked hard to instill a passion for customer service among its employees. It used to give new employees their employee handbook on a single five-by-eight inch card containing the following:[43]

Welcome to Nordstrom

We're glad to have you with our company. Our number one goal is to provide outstanding customer service. Set both your personal and professional goals high. We have great confidence in your ability to achieve them.

Nordstrom Rules: Rule #1: Use good judgment in all situations. There will be no additional rules.

Please feel free to ask your department manager, store manager, or division general manager any question at any time.

Nordstrom built passion around their central message to be great at customer service.

For many of us, passion is not something we are born with—we develop our passions. Passion plays an important role in innovation

---

43 http://en.wikipedia.org/wiki/Nordstrom.

because it frames the fundamentals that drive innovation decisions. Nordstrom felt it could grow its customer relationships by creating a passion for customer service among its employees. They believed that the passion would manifest itself in every customer interaction and, by being passionate, they would instill in customers the idea that Nordstrom is all about great service.

$ Every CEO needs to determine the right passion for the company. Whatever that passion is, it is very important to align individual passions with the company passions. When you decide what your colleagues should be passionate about, communicating it as simply as Nordstrom's Rule #1. To get employees truly passionate about the goal, link their personal values to that goal, just as Toyota did at NUMMI. Then link people together in teams that rally around that shared personal goal.

Rewards

Jack Trytten wrote a wonderful book titled *The Failure of Marketing*. Go to Amazon.com or Jack's Web site http://failureofmarketing.com/ and look at the picture. This is the image to keep in mind when thinking about setting up a bonus structure for innovation teams. It is a clever photo of a man shooting himself in the foot.

Ideas about measuring and rewarding innovation through a bonus structure have become more frequent subjects recently in articles about innovation. Beyond measuring innovation broadly in terms of long-term business success, the evidence for the value of such measurement is unconvincing. If you truly have people engaged and empowered, they are going to be innovative and seek excellence in doing so. Overlaying a lot of reporting requirements on people should only be done with a good business reason in mind. If the purpose of measuring innovation and problem solving is to show its value, then what is the point? Everyone already knows it's valuable. The best thing a leader can do in that circumstance is to get out of the way.

As was evident in the book's accompanying case, anytime you establish a reward based on a measurement, you open yourself up to employees gaming the measurement, and you get unforeseen consequences. Problem solving and invention are basic human activities.[44] We are naturally good at them, and that is why we dominate the earth. The key is to align personal values with the company goals—that's how you motivate innovation. Rewarding a natural activity doesn't motivate it. You can reward people for breathing, but it is not likely to change their breathing activity much. About the only control you can have over breathing is to stop it. The same is true of problem solving and invention. The only real control you have over it is to stop it. Don't worry about rewarding it; worry about stopping it.

---

44 Problem solving and invention are not the same thing as innovation. Innovation is about creating competitive advantage for the company by implementing ideas acquired through problem solving and invention. Problem solving and invention are such natural activities that they go on in spite of any management activity. The problem with a culture that's not conducive to trust and engagement is that most of these solutions and inventions never get out of the brain of their creators. Unless that happens, there's no innovation. And that's why there is so much frustration in those types of companies. In such companies, surveys have shown senior executives tend to believe they don't have the right people on board to innovate, while people below them believe they have the right people, just the wrong culture.

Aside from not being a significant motivator for innovation, financial rewards have the potential to go wrong. A large bank had a practice of rewarding innovation teams based on the imputed value of the innovation delivered. The intention was good, the result—well they shot themselves in the foot. First, the rewards were distributed for any team-based problem solving—it didn't have to be innovative. That is, the team could be addressing an internal problem that had nothing to do with creating competitive advantage.

Second, it left off people who were not officially on the team. In many projects, there were people who played key roles but couldn't be released from their demanding day jobs to be assigned to the team, so they didn't share in the reward. Occasionally, there were people who were not on the team and who played only a quick role, but in doing so provided the key insight or even the solution to the problem. They, too, didn't share the reward. Additionally, any time people are pulled away from their normal responsibilities to work on an innovation project, someone has to fill in for them. Those people also support the innovation effort. They provide the extra effort to make sure the normal day-to-day work still gets done, but they also are left out of the reward structure.

The problem here is that, usually, your best problem solvers do it for the joy of problem solving and for the recognition of their cleverness. When they don't share in the reward, then they don't get that recognition, and their contribution is overlooked. Before that moment, their contribution was a positive experience, but the reward structure turned it into a negative one. They start to disengage.

Third, people gamed the system. Steven Levitt talks about the impact of high-stakes standardized testing on teacher behavior in his book *Freakonomics*. In many states, rules around how mandatory standardized test scores would determine the fate of schools, administrators, teachers, and students provided incentives for teachers to manipulate the system. In one case, a teacher engaged in bold-faced cheating by writing the correct answers on the chalkboard. In other cases, the activity was more subtle such as giving students more time to complete the test or teaching students the specific material covered by the test questions or basing lessons on last year's test or (because only correct answers were counted) instructing students to fill in all remaining multiple choice blanks in the last few seconds of the test. Some of the cheating strategies were quite creative, and I encourage you to read *Freakonomics*. If you want to reward innovation, be precise in determining what behavior you want to incent, and if some people game the system, change the system.

$ If your workforce is fully engaged, you do not need to incent them to solve problems. But if you feel that rewarding innovation is important, recognize that there is no way to be sure you are including all contributors within the company unless you include everyone in the company. Just share the wealth. Executed well, rewarding equally across the board for innovation can be a good thing. One way to do it is to establish a way to track revenue streams from new innovations and distribute them using a model that says something like: in its first full year in the market, 25 percent of net profits from an innovation will go into this innovation bonus pool. First year profits are often pretty small. In the second full year, 15 percent of profits go into the pool, and in the third year, 5 percent of profits go into the pool.

Distribute the pool equally among all employees at the end of each year. This encourages everyone to support each other's innovation efforts and not to shy away from big challenges.

Problem-Solving Teams

Cross-functional teams are very useful. Typically, these teams are good at solving problems. A team is always able to generate more ideas than a single individual. The trick for competitive advantage isn't generating lots of ideas. Rather, the trick is selecting the best idea. Teams often end up compromising on their solutions. Where change is involved, consensus tends to favor the middle of the road.

Recently, I had a discussion with a fellow innovation author who claimed he could put together any cross-functional team in a company, and they would solve any problem the company faced. I agreed that was probably true. I then asked him to identify a breakthrough innovation that such a team had created. He thought for a few moments, tried a couple of examples, and then stopped, realizing that either the innovation wasn't much of a breakthrough or that the team was implementing an idea it was given. "Well," he said. "I'm sure one will come to mind if I think about it."

I am still waiting.

Why then, is it that most breakthrough ideas do not often come from such teams? We did a survey asking people to identify a breakthrough innovation that was born in a cross-functional team. Everyone who responded could come up with examples of cross-functional teams creating good solutions to problems, or a cross-functional team being good at implementing a breakthrough idea. But not one person could come up with an example of a cross-functional team coming up with a breakthrough idea. Whereas everyone could identify breakthrough ideas created by an individual. That's not to say that there are no examples of cross-functional teams inventing a breakthrough. It is just harder to come up with a ready example.

If you've been reading this book sequentially, you probably have some insight into why this might be true. Let's go through the environment of a typical cross-functional team.

In cross-functional teams, you bring together experts, and often these are people steeped in the *way things are done around here*. They do help each other to be more open-minded because they bring different points of view to the table, but each of them is burdened by the mindset biases created by their repeated exposure to the current solutions, by their familiarity with "how it's done around here," and by the status quo. In other words, they will be more likely to reject an idea to solve the problem if the idea means a lot of change or it is greatly different from what's done today.

Experts tend to be very good devil's advocates. As we've discussed, change is always an affront to the way our brains work. If you are an expert in the problem area, then the solution always involves change. The bigger the change, the more objections experts can produce, and those objections are usually couched as reasons why something won't work. It is about killing the idea, not exploring it further.

The key question is: can you construct a team that is more likely to come up with breakthrough ideas than your typical cross-functional team? The answer is yes. We call it a *cross-talented* team. The difference is whom you include on the team.

A handful of years ago, I was managing a cross-talented team that had the mundane assignment to review the functionality of a computer system supporting the authorization process in a credit card business. We were taking advantage of the fact that the underlying operating system was being retired, and we would need to port the authorization system to a new platform. Since the computer code would have to be rewritten anyway, we thought we'd take advantage of the opportunity to fine-tune the system's functionality.

I put together the team made up of experts from the technology team, experts from the authorization groups, along with a couple of project managers, and one supersynthesizer who had little exposure to the authorization process in the business. In that narrow sense, he was a novice. The team members came into a hotel meeting room in Rome from various parts of the world.

We started on Sunday evening. By Tuesday afternoon, the team had divided itself into two camps, each favoring a different approach. The two approaches were not compatible, and we would have to choose one. We were at an impasse.

That evening, the supersynthesizer approached me and asked if he and I could have dinner together. Over dinner, he meticulously took me through his understanding of the two approaches and why they were incompatible. He outlined the parts of each that he thought best addressed the problem but acknowledged that either would provide the authorization functionality to meet the business process requirements as defined. Next, he tackled the process definition itself and explained that it was not necessarily the best approach to the risk-management purpose for which it was designed. He had an alternative. Then he took bits and pieces from each of the two proposed solutions and came up with a system design that would deliver against his alternative process definition.

It took the better part of two days to let the other members of the team understand the idea, object to it, and finally embrace it. It was a business model change and a breakthrough innovation that delivered a 10 percent lift in annual sales worldwide.

What allowed this to happen was a team structure that leveraged the knowledge of the experts and the brain of a supersynthesizer who carried no heavy bias as to *how things are done* today.

$ A cross-talented team is made up of the experts who bring knowledge and experience, one or two novice supersynthesizers (not more—three would be too disruptive[45]) who bring the fresh capable minds to the problem and ask the interesting "stupid" questions, and a couple of project management types, one of whom will take the lead in project delivery. By including the project manager in the earliest stage of the team, you expose him or her to the deep thinking that defined the problem and crafted the solution. With that back-

---

45 Including multiple supersynthesizers can be very interesting when you are doing blue-sky ideation like Nathan Myhrvold does at Intellectual Ventures, where the goal is to develop a large patent portfolio rather than to actually develop any product. The discussion can easily go far afield of the original problem and end up focusing on distant, unrelated problems instead.

ground, the project manager will be well positioned to deal with obstacles that inevitably come along so that the final delivery matches the problem precisely.

Managing a cross-talented team can be more challenging than managing a cross-functional team, but the results are always better.

The purpose of this little book was not to point out something as trivial as competitive advantage is obtained by solving a customer's problem better than the competition. Or that continuous innovation is how we sustain competitive advantage. Rather, the purpose of this book is to create a chain of causality through a chain of reasoning that points us to what is foundational to being the competitive powerhouse in your industry.

Solving problems is the key talent needed to sustain competitive advantage. Two kinds of problem solving are needed. First, regular problem solving deals with issues that contribute to the company's ability to deliver, but these are not problems that directly differentiate the company from the competition for the customer. These are problems in accounting, finance, operations, systems, human resources, and other support functions for which the solution can be a common solution across many industries or across businesses within your industry. These problems do not require you to create new knowledge. You can use any good existing solution.

Where you want competitive advantage, however, you must solve the customer problem in a way that the competition cannot easily copy. For that, you need to create new knowledge. It can be tacit knowledge that you hold close to the vest. Or it can be new knowledge that you can protect through intellectual property law. Such knowledge can keep the competition from copying your advantage.

Humans create new knowledge in three ways. Discovery, experimentation, and synthesis are the ways we create new knowledge, although individual instances of knowledge creation often use more than one of these methods simultaneously. In ancient times, discovery was the primary means by which humans created new knowledge. With the coming of the Age of Reason, that transitioned into experimentation. Today, we rely more on synthesis, which builds on existing knowledge and combines it in new ways to create new knowledge.

I showed in the text that there are people who, like Richard Feynman, are extraordinarily good at synthesis. If you can identify these people, they can add value in particular ways within the company. They are very good at understanding how problems fit into the big picture and how elements in the proposed solution fit or do not fit the problem. Using these talented people individually for specific tough problems, or on cross-talented teams, adds significantly to a company's ability to create competitive advantage.

But they are not the only problem solvers in the company. Examples like the NUMMI automobile assembly plant drive home the truth that virtually anyone is a capable problem solver. The truth is, sometimes the most useful insight comes from an unlikely place in the organization. You don't want to miss that opportunity. All problem solvers benefit from elastic brains. Encouraging the workforce to expand their knowledge into new areas increases their brain elasticity and provides a richer base for finding metaphors that help identify problems and solutions.

We are all problem solvers. The real leadership question is: are the employees solving problems for our business, or are they consumed with surviving company politics and intrigue? It is hard to engage employees in solving problems for the company if other non-related challenges dominate their lives.

To be the competitive powerhouse the new normal calls for, you must have everyone in the company engaged in problem solving and innovating. The workforce must be highly engaged. That takes extraordinary leadership. Leadership creates that engagement. But engagement doesn't take hold in environments where trust is in question. Two-way trust is foundational. But more important, and more difficult for a leader to do, is to empower people to pursue problem solving in ways they think are best.

I mentioned several instances where important innovations met with stiff resistance from the CEO. In those examples, the companies were fortunate to have persistent, independent-minded employees, who carried on in spite of their bosses. Books have been written about how to be one of those heroic internal entrepreneurs who persevered despite enormous bureaucratic obstacles to deliver real value to the company.

Relying on heroes is a failure of leadership. To be the powerhouse of innovation, the leader knows the value of every brain at work in the company. Engaging these brains is the CEO's fundamental responsibility.

What is blameworthy in those bosses is that they relied on their gut. But the gut is really the brain, and the brain is plagued with bias and a phenomenon commonly called being too close to the problem.

If you're going to lead a competitive powerhouse, you need to realize that the best idea you'll ever hear will sound idiotic at first. Luis Filipe Reis at Sonaecom know this. As does Robert Galvin at Motorola. Both Robert Galvin and Luis Filipe Reis understood that their first judgment does not always recognize the full value of a new idea. Likewise both leaders established mechanisms to allow good ideas to bubble to the surface. When he ran Motorola, Galvin put in place a process that automatically allowed an employee to advance an idea to some action. At Sonaecom, the idea marketplace ensures that many brains are looking at ideas, and it only takes a small subset of employee *investors* to drive a good idea forward.

By building trust and empowering employees, you enable engagement. You make the engagement take hold by linking the work an employee does to her sense of self and her drive to make the world a better place. If the work allows people to prove their worth to themselves, you have a winning formula. Then build small teams of such people with that as their common bond. They will produce the internal motivation that will enable the company to dominate in its industry. **G**reat **O**rganizational **L**eaders **F**acilitate **T**rust, **E**ngagement, and **E**mpowerment (GOLF TEE™). This gives everyone in the company the ability to strive for excellence. It enables the company to be the competitive powerhouse in its industry.

Final word: The *new normal* will put additional pressure on companies to create competitive advantage. If consumer spending is done more carefully in the future, then being good at understanding customer problems and solving them is critical to advantage and prosperity.

CASE STUDY—PROBLEM SOLVING IN THE BACK OFFICE

The following case is a real-world, practical illustration of a number of the ideas covered in the text of this book. (Names are fictional.)

Case Abstract:

The chargeback unit of a large merchant processing bank on the West Coast had a significant, overwhelming operating problem. For the past year, it had suffered an ongoing annual operating loss. For the kind of processing the department performed, it should not have taken any loss at all. Here, at the end of May, the annual loss run rate had gradually grown to $8 million. But the problem had resisted all attempts to fix it.

At the time, it was losing $8 million per year; the chargeback department was the largest such operation in the world. It employed 120 people organized into five sections.

Fred Schmidt is the senior vice president for the card business, which employed over 5,000 people at the time. Fred had been in his job for three years, having come to California from a large New York-based bank. He was known as a thoughtful but action-oriented leader who could work effectively with all levels of people in his organization. He'd been brought in to institute better controls and to ensure that

Fred Schmidt
SVP Card Business

the business units were profitable as stand-alone operations.

Gerry Khan manages the back office operations center for the merchant card business. It is one of the business units within the card business and employs over 800 people. Gerry has been with the bank for thirty years. He started in the mail room and worked his way up. He reports to Fred Schmidt

Gerry Khan
VP Merchant
Center Mngr

Reporting to Gerry is **Sarah Macintosh** who has overall management responsibility for the 120 people in the chargeback department. Sarah has been in the role for five years. Until last year, no significant problems had arisen and the occasional backlog never generated an annual operating loss greater than $100,000.

Sarah Macintosh
VP Chargeback
Processing

Over the past several months, Sarah had found herself in meetings with both Gerry and Mr. Schmidt to discuss the problems in the chargeback unit. About a year ago, a backlog developed at the same time a 10 percent spike developed in the number of chargebacks, as the sales group had brought a large airline into the business. During the following four months, three other large airlines were added to the business, resulting in an additional 25 percent increase in chargebacks.

To compensate for this increase in volume, the number of chargeback clerks was increased from seventy to 120 people, organized into the five sections, each with a supervisor who reported to Sarah.

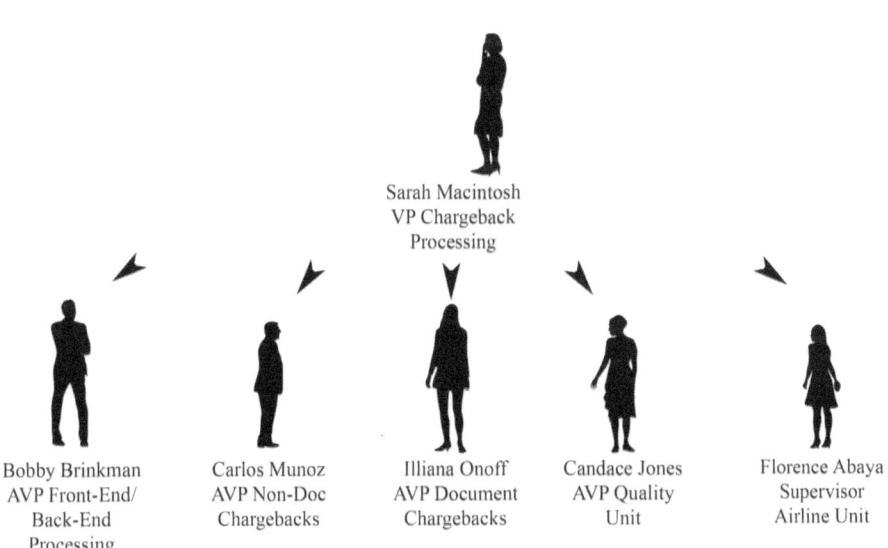

When a new chargeback first arrived, it went to the front end, where a file folder was created and an accounting entry was made. Nondocument chargebacks were delivered daily from the front end to the nondoc chargeback section for work. If the chargeback indicated that documentation was to follow, then the file would be sent either to Illiana in the document chargeback section or, if it was an airline charge, it would go to the airline unit.

Documentation could arrive automatically from the issuer, or it could arrive from the merchant, when a chargeback clerk had requested supporting documentation from the merchant. In either case, the documentation was put in a hanging folder, a label would be made with the card account number and placed on the folder, and then the folder would be hung on a rack in account number order. Whenever a clerk was working a chargeback file that was waiting for documentation, he or she would check the rack to see if documentation had arrived for that account number.

Bobby Brinkman managed the front end/back end. He'd come to this job two months ago from the finance department. Viewed as an up and comer, he'd requested a job that would give him operations management experience since he'd already worked in credit and in financial control. He'd only been with the bank less than a year but had made some changes in the financial control area that had gotten Fred Schmidt's attention. He was considered the most knowledgeable person in the back office when it came to Card Association regulations, as he had read all the manuals in his attempt to learn the business. Gerry, the center manager, would call on Bobby whenever questions came up regarding regulations. Personally, Bobby was astounded that he was the only person in the 800 person center who'd actually thoroughly read the regulations.

Carlos Munoz started in the chargeback department eight years before as a front-end clerk. He'd gradually worked his way through every clerk job and eventually was made a supervisor in the document chargeback group. Three years ago, when the assistant vice president nondoc chargeback job became open he was promoted to that role, getting the AVP title and a parking place in the building a year after that. Carlos was well liked by his team and seemed to know everyone in the building. If you needed something done, Carlos could tell you whom to contact.

Illiana was a Russian refugee who'd sought asylum in the United States. She'd been working for the bank for ten years, including six in the chargeback department, which she joined as the AVP of charge-back processing. She had a PhD in chemistry and had been a research scientist at a pharmaceutical company in Russia before escaping. Illiana spoke English with a heavy accent. Often it seemed she could barely discuss an issue under consideration, until somehow the other person found he was boxed in by her points. She was smart, meticu-lous, strict, and highly organized. There was never a backlog in her section. Sarah liked her, as did Bobby Brinkman, but everybody else avoided her.

Florence Abaya was a Filipina who'd come to the United States with her husband on their honeymoon and had never left. She'd been a chargeback clerk for five years before becoming supervisor of the Airline Unit when it was created. Florence was expecting her fifth child and would be off work in a month on maternity leave. The airline unit was her first supervisory role. Some of the operating loss came from this group. Sarah was very concerned about Florence's impending maternity leave, as Florence seemed to be doing half the work her-self. Florence was always the first one into the office in the morning and the last one out at night. On any Saturday you could find Florence putting in a full day of work. As a devout Catholic, Florence would not work on Sundays, but she made up for it every Monday and Tuesday by putting in sixteen-hour days. As hard as she worked, the unit always seemed to be behind. Recently, Sarah had added three more people to Airline Unit, hoping to get on top of the backlog.

By far the biggest portion of the loss came from the Quality Unit. **Candace Jones** celebrated her twentieth anniversary with the bank a year ago. She'd worked in various junior manager roles for the past ten years and came to the chargeback department eighteen months ago to establish a quality program for the department as part of a companywide initiative. When Sarah reorganized the overall chargeback department late last year, she created the quality unit and put Candace in charge. Candace was a single mother of four children. The oldest was graduating from high school in less than a month, and headed to Stanford with a full scholarship in the fall. Candace seemed to flip back and forth from extremely proud mother to manic supervisor all day long. Sarah had confided to Gerry that she was worried Candace would snap under the pressure. Gerry knew Candace's history and was not worried; she'd faced much bigger challenges in her personal life than anything the workplace could dish out.

In addition to the supervisors, reporting to Sarah was Seymour Goldfarb, the senior MIS analyst for the department. Seymour had two junior analysts who reported to him. The three of them produced a volume of MIS reports every evening that focused primarily on the losses.

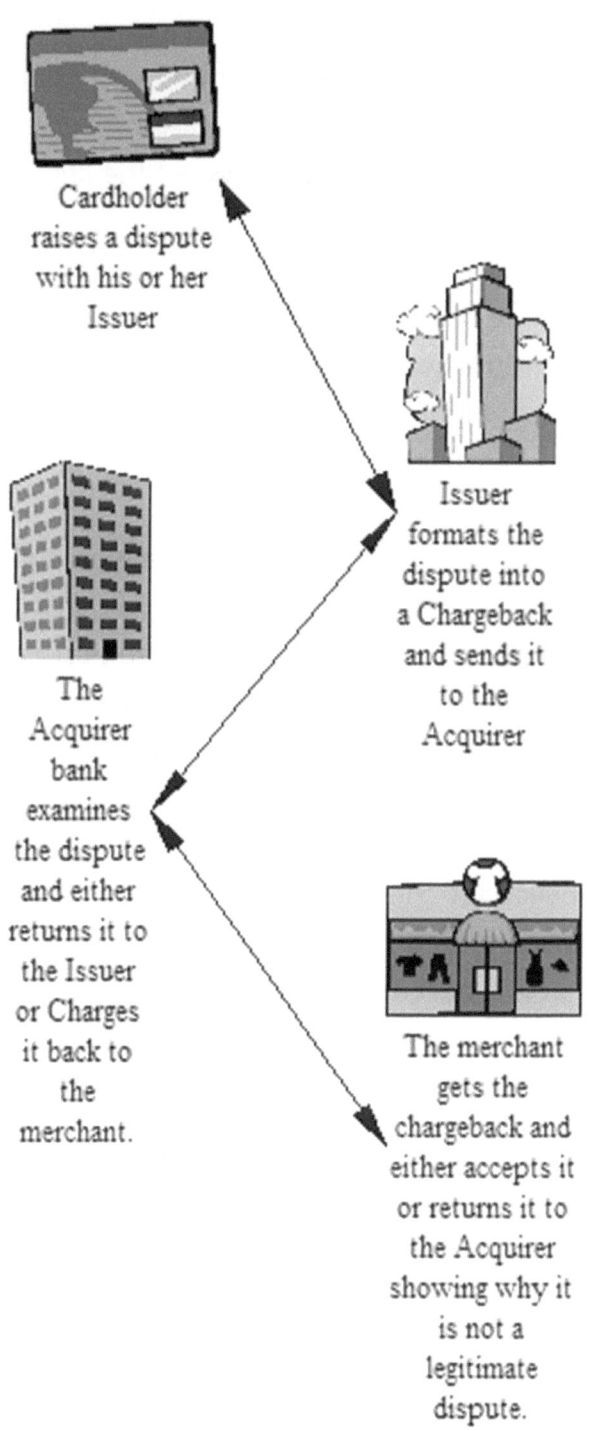

Cardholder raises a dispute with his or her Issuer

Issuer formats the dispute into a Chargeback and sends it to the Acquirer

The Acquirer bank examines the dispute and either returns it to the Issuer or Charges it back to the merchant.

The merchant gets the chargeback and either accepts it or returns it to the Acquirer showing why it is not a legitimate dispute.

A chargeback is simply a dispute between a cardholder and a merchant. The dispute always originates with the cardholder and is initiated with the cardholder's bank. The cardholder's bank is called *the issuer* because it is the bank that issued the credit card to the customer.

The dispute can be raised for any number of different reasons: the cardholder claims the goods were never received or were defective; the charge was a duplicate; the amount was incorrect; or it was a fraud transaction not done by the cardholder.

The issuer collects the necessary documentation supporting the cardholder's claim and formats an electronic chargeback transaction. As this transaction is processed through the credit-card association, it credits the disputed amount back to the issuer and charges it back to the bank that originally acquired the transaction from the merchant (*the acquirer*).

The acquirer receives the documentation, examines it to determine the apparent legitimacy of the claim, and decides whether or not to charge it back to the merchant. If it gets charged back to the merchant, the merchant, in turn, determines whether the claim is correct and either accepts it or represents the charge to its acquirer.

The acquirer then sends the representation back to the issuer and on to the cardholder.

The dispute can go through a couple of cycles of this back-and-forth routing without being resolved. At the final cycle, the acquirer is always left with the charge.

The acquirer's last resort is to send the chargeback case to the card association for mandatory arbitration. The card association will then resolve the dispute and charge the losing party a significant processing fee.

Sarah Macintosh's Description of the Chargeback Workflow

The issuer sends the chargeback to the association. The association performs some edits on the data to make sure the chargeback is valid, and then sends it on to the acquirer (that's us). In the front end/back end unit Bobby's people create a case for each chargeback and create the paper accounting entries. These accounting entries are taken upstairs to the accounting department every day before 2:00 P.M.

The case folders are then sent to a table in the processing shop where either Carlos or Illiana separate them into airline and nonairline groups, and then into document and nondocument groups. Carlos takes the nondoc pile and adds them to his inventory for distribution the next day. Illiana takes the document chargebacks. Florence gets all the airline chargebacks.

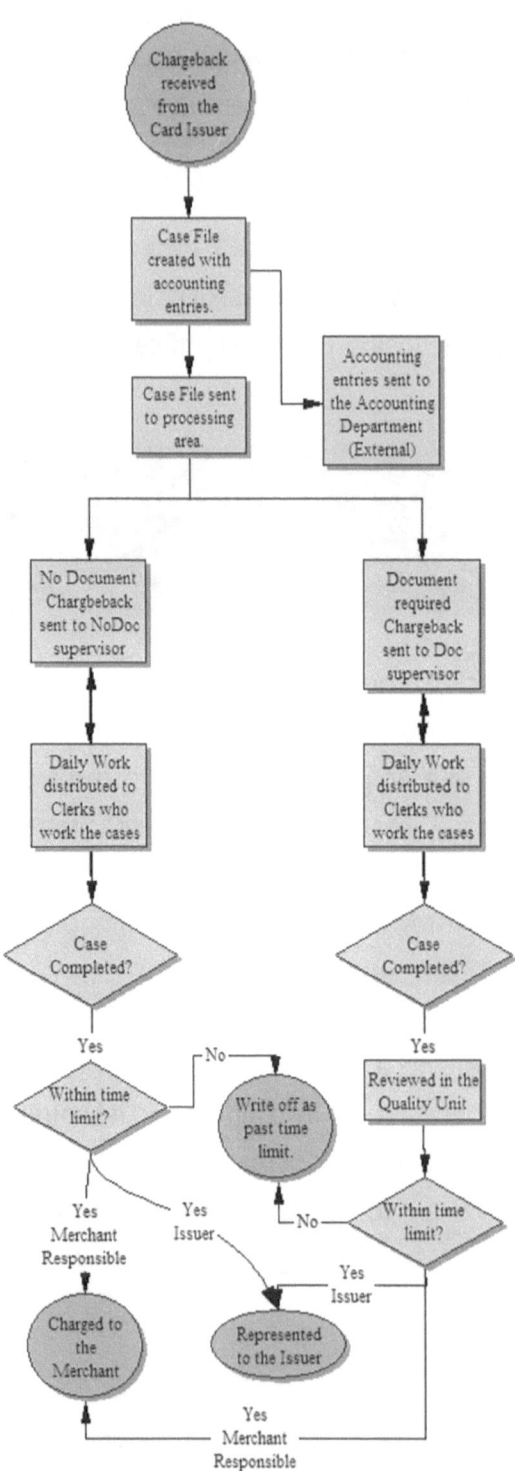

Every morning, the files are randomly distributed into the same number of piles as there are clerks in the unit. Document files go to the doc clerks because they are our more experienced clerks. Each clerk gets more files than they usually can do in a day; in the past, there have been occasions when a nondoc clerk finished all his work and needed to find more. But for the most part, each clerk has some files left over at the end of the day.

Document cases can be quite complex and have all kinds of supporting paperwork. Often, there is a need to go out to the merchant to get additional information, and all this takes time. This is what can cause a case to go past time and go to loss.

Completed cases go out of the unit. Doc cases (both airline and non-airline) go to the quality unit. Once they are reviewed, they are resolved and sent either back to the issuer or charged to the merchant through the back end.

The back end handles the accounting.

MIS delivered on 14 May

Non-Airline Chargeback Cases
Incomming Volume Report 13 May
Month

Chargeback Reason Code	Actual Jan	Actual Feb	Actual Mar	Actual Apr	MTD May	Plan Jun	Plan Jul	Plan Aug	Plan Sep	Plan Oct	Plan Nov	Plan Dec
Requested copy not received	4564	4791	4768	4570	4855	2965	2948	3033	2944	3020	3030	2923
Requested copy illegible or missing	334	383	328	349	384	394	391	403	389	400	403	388
Warning bulletin listing	391	374	365	365	387	394	391	403	389	400	403	388
Not Authorized	809	954	916	857	927	985	979	1008	974	1002	1007	971
Account not on file	179	164	195	167	198	197	195	201	194	200	201	194
Wrong Amount	394	340	342	385	338	394	391	403	389	400	403	388
Duplicate	168	186	174	160	183	197	195	201	194	200	201	194
Card expired/invalid	707	702	767	678	781	788	783	806	779	801	806	776
No cardholder authorization	1374	1123	1309	1180	1204	1379	1370	1411	1364	1403	1410	1359
Fraudulent transaction	891	837	844	944	872	985	979	1008	974	1002	1007	971
Canceled recurring transaction	192	197	185	182	159	197	195	201	194	200	201	194
Late presentment	2292	2130	1897	2230	1993	2365	2349	2419	2339	2405	2418	2330
Wrong currency	1069	1027	980	991	1130	1182	1174	1209	1169	1202	1209	1165
Exceeds floor limit fraudulent	1836	1802	1873	1889	2010	2168	2153	2217	2144	2205	2216	2136
Fraud merchant	929	979	922	835	958	985	979	1008	974	1002	1007	971
Credit posted as a debit	165	163	157	180	162	197	195	201	194	200	201	194
Non-receipt of services	1054	1083	1098	1155	979	1182	1174	1209	1169	1202	1209	1165
Merchandise defective or not as described	733	678	715	684	691	788	783	806	779	801	806	776
Fraud—Card-Absent Environment	683	770	634	703	651	788	783	806	779	801	806	776
Credit Not Processed	361	387	354	318	337	394	391	403	389	400	403	388
Paid by Other Means	584	541	550	486	519	591	587	604	584	801	604	582

Airline Chargeback Cases
Incomming Volume Report 13 May
Month

Chargeback Reason Code	Actual Jan	Actual Feb	Actual Mar	Actual Apr	MTD May	Plan Jun	Plan Jul	Plan Aug	Plan Sep	Plan Oct	Plan Nov	Plan Dec
Requested copy not received	1537	1668	1530	1601	1671	1637	1562	1575	1678	1432	1726	1698
Requested copy illegible or missing	249	222	235	223	268	242	250	238	251	225	255	233
Warning bulletin listing	112	113	111	114	109	106	125	123	129	126	124	119
Not Authorized	321	302	269	292	271	272	264	300	305	329	276	310
Account not on file	213	262	247	257	257	245	250	237	216	242	236	239
Wrong Amount	122	116	129	126	110	107	112	108	118	110	108	114
Duplicate	62	62	57	54	56	60	59	58	53	60	59	54
Card expired/invalid	250	262	233	236	247	250	215	230	253	231	209	220
No cardholder authorization	635	582	609	549	622	573	597	579	533	651	552	596
Fraudulent transaction	271	317	324	270	320	298	304	323	292	324	264	308
Canceled recurring transaction	1	2	2	2	2	2	1	1	2	2	1	2
Late presentment	119	108	126	123	120	122	104	133	114	131	107	129
Wrong currency	129	116	112	123	115	122	117	112	120	129	123	123
Exceeds floor limit fraudulent	292	302	264	316	335	279	272	319	295	329	277	303
Fraud merchant	12	12	12	12	12	11	11	11	12	10	12	12
Credit posted as a debit	53	62	53	61	55	59	53	66	56	57	55	60
Non-receipt of services	840	693	782	801	775	776	810	842	812	813	717	695
Merchandise defective or not as described	249	221	212	260	224	263	234	243	210	219	231	239
Fraud—Card-Absent Environment	482	467	508	470	491	425	500	449	434	509	439	515
Credit Not Processed	332	350	352	352	358	388	319	348	338	360	373	350
Paid by Other Means	313	305	273	281	283	329	295	317	267	316	287	266
Non-Receipt of Cash at ATM	59	57	59	60	55	56	55	56	57	54	55	59

MIS delivered on 14 May

Airline Chargeback Cases — Incoming Volume Report 13 May

Chargeback Type	Actual Jan	Actual Feb	Actual Mar	Actual Apr	MTD May	Plan Jun	Plan Jul	Plan Aug	Plan Sep	Plan Oct	Plan Nov	Plan Dec
No Document Chargebacks	2843	2977	2782	2926	3031	2903	2827	2925	2988	2814	3001	3031
Document Chargebacks	3810	3624	3717	3657	3725	3719	3682	3743	3557	3845	3485	3613
Total	6653	6601	6499	6583	6756	6622	6509	6668	6545	6659	6486	6644

Non-Airline Chargeback Cases — Incomming Volume Report 13 May

Chargeback Type	Actual Jan	Actual Feb	Actual Mar	Actual Apr	MTD May	Plan Jun	Plan Jul	Plan Aug	Plan Sep	Plan Oct	Plan Nov	Plan Dec
No Document Chargebacks	10405	10598	10342	10427	10754	9468	9406	9684	9373	9632	9678	9330
Document Chargebacks	9471	9198	9212	9047	9129	10244	10174	10477	10125	10415	10474	10093
Total	19876	19796	19554	19474	19883	19712	19580	20161	19498	20047	20152	19423

Total Chargeback Cases — Incomming Volume Report 13 May

Chargeback Type	Actual Jan	Actual Feb	Actual Mar	Actual Apr	MTD May	Plan Jun	Plan Jul	Plan Aug	Plan Sep	Plan Oct	Plan Nov	Plan Dec
No Document Chargebacks	13248	13575	13124	13353	13785	12371	12233	12609	12361	12446	12679	12361
Document Chargebacks	13281	12822	12929	12704	12854	13963	13856	14220	13682	14260	13959	13706
Total	26529	26397	26053	26057	26639	26334	26089	26829	26043	26706	26638	26067

Total Chargeback Cases — Incomming Volume Report 13 May

Chargeback Source	Actual Jan	Actual Feb	Actual Mar	Actual Apr	MTD May	Plan Jun	Plan Jul	Plan Aug	Plan Sep	Plan Oct	Plan Nov	Plan Dec

Backlog and Loss Inventory

# Cases	0	15 days	30 days	45	more than	Write
Inventory Aging as of 13 May	15 days	30 days	45 days	60 days	60 days	Off
Non-Airline Chargeback Cases						
No Document Chargebacks	4839	4692	4654	4769	4682	21273
Document Chargebacks	4108	4071	4145	4139	4262	18653
Airline Chargeback Cases						
No Document Chargebacks	1364	1317	1252	1340	1279	5896
Document Chargebacks	1676	1646	1673	1631	1715	7505

						YTD
$ Volume	0	15 days	30 days	45	more than	Write
Inventory Aging as of 13 May	15 days	30 days	45 days	60 days	60 days	Off
Non-Airline Chargeback Cases						
No Document Chargebacks	194302	202070	200628	204434	193774	870139
Document Chargebacks	225700	260577	260005	245370	223045	1094146
Airline Chargeback Cases						
No Document Chargebacks	94245	87410	82278	90546	76328	429304
Document Chargebacks	273715	326910	312489	316179	334804	1341179
						3734768

If a chargeback ages past forty-five days, it can no longer be represented to the issuer through the association. The association actually has a system edit that blocks the transaction. Any time a case reaches forty days, it gets included in the backlog database. The location of the file is often unknown, as it will be in someone's work pile. All the chargeback clerks have instructions to work those file as a priority.

Once a chargeback goes past forty-five days it is *past time frame* and is disposed of in one of three ways.

1. It can be a chargeback to the merchant where the merchant is responsible for the underlying dispute. (The

exception is for a couple of the big airline accounts with which the bank has a special relationship. These two contracts forbid any chargebacks to the airline 110 days after the transaction date. Because travel is often well after the date the airline ticket is purchased, lots of time can pass before something happens that results in a dispute. By the time it is processed in the chargeback unit, it is over 110 days old.)

2. It can be sent back to the issuer using a process called good-faith collection. In this case, the issuer can choose to accept the collection case and attempt to collect from the cardholder or reject the case. Only when the cardholder accepts responsibility for the charge will the issuer pay us. Only about 5 percent of these get collected.

3. If it cannot be otherwise disposed of we write it off as a loss. Most past time-frame chargebacks end up getting written off.

The current annual run rate on losses is just over $8 million. This is consistent with the run rate at the end of last year.

Resolution

Around the end of March, Bobby Brinkman began making suggestions during the daily managers meeting with Sarah Macintosh and her other direct reports. At first, Sarah was fairly patient with his well-intentioned suggestions. In fact, she allowed him to implement a few of his ideas. He bought a couple of PCs and added bar-code readers to them, and then he printed unique bar code labels that he attached to the files. This allowed him to track the file in his front end/back end department. He then created a little program that printed out the accounting slip using incoming association data downloaded from the mainframe. When a file came back to the back end, a clerk could scan its barcode and automatically create the accounting slip that would take it out of suspense and charge it either to the merchant or the issuer. Since he had to sign each of the 2,400 entries that were processed on the average day, she even allowed him to have a rubber stamp made with his signature, but that only lasted until someone told the internal auditors that Bobby was using a rubber stamp. They put a stop to that. Sarah felt good about that. She'd given him a little rope, and although he hadn't hung himself, he'd probably learned his lesson to be more cautious before making any more changes.

When Bobby started to make suggestions about processing ideas for areas outside his front end/back end, she felt she needed to rein him in. On one occasion, he suggested they use the barcodes on the files to track which clerk was working on a file. But Sarah pointed out that it wouldn't really add any value since, at the beginning of each day, the files were redistributed, and the file would then be assigned to a different clerk to work. Bobby suggested that perhaps once a file was assigned to a clerk, that clerk should be responsible for the file until it was resolved. No, explained Sarah, that also would not work, aside from the fact that documentation is often still not in for the case, but also you could not tell how much work a particular file would take. One clerk could end up with a lot of hard cases, while another ended up with a bunch of easy ones. And that would not allow them to fairly measure productivity, which was how the clerks' performance was measured.

Bobby suggested that they renegotiate the two airline contracts with the 110-day clauses, so the bank wouldn't have to take those losses. Sarah pointed out that there was a bigger bank relationship with those two merchants, and they were very important bank customers. The chairman of the bank had once sat on one of the airline's board of directors.

Bobby suggested that perhaps they should just assign an individual clerk to an individual chargeback reason code and hold that clerk responsible for that inventory. Again, Sarah pointed out that each reason code could be more, or less, complex or difficult than every other reason code. It would prevent the business from establishing production standards that would be fair to everyone. Bobby suggested that perhaps there was another way to gauge performance. She pointed out that the bank used a forced-ranking system, and they needed to place the clerks according to that model across the five performance levels.

At this point, Sarah suggested to Bobby that she appreciated his enthusiasm, but the things he suggested had been tried in the past or were just unworkable. Perhaps, she cautioned, he should keep his thoughts to himself until he'd been in the department a while longer and had a better understanding of how things worked.

Unknown to either Sarah or Bobby, Illiana Onoff went home every evening and told her husband about these exchanges between Bobby and Sarah. Illiana complained that she thought some of Bobby's ideas were good ideas, and they should be tried. Illiana's husband also worked in the center, and he relayed his wife's comments to his boss, Jason Hazzard. Jason occasionally played tennis with Gerry Chan, the center manager. On one such occasion, the topic of the losses in the chargeback unit came up and Jason told Gerry about Bobby's ideas.

On the next Monday morning, Gerry called Bobby up to the fifth floor for a conference. Gerry told Bobby that what they shared would be confidential, but he wanted to hear Bobby's ideas for making changes in the chargeback unit. At the end of the conference, Gerry asked Bobby to put together a presentation outlining his ideas. Although Bobby believed Gerry might just be patronizing him, he had no choice but to write the presentation and give it to Gerry. Later, on Friday, he received a call from Gerry. "Practice your presentation over the weekend," he instructed. "At 10:00 A.M. on Monday, you and I are headed downtown to meet with Fred Schmidt, senior vice president of the Card Business."

Bobby was nervous when he started the presentation, but when Fred asked a couple of good questions, he gained confidence. At the end of Bobby's presentation, Fred leaned back in his big leather chair, laced his fingertips together, and brought them to his chin. He was silent for a few minutes. Then he looked Bobby in the eye. "If you'd started your presentation with the idea that you'd eliminate the backlog, you'd cut losses to near zero, and you'd do it with half the people, I think I would have thrown you out of the office," Fred said. Then he smiled. "But, now that I understand what you're proposing, I think you should take a shot at it. I don't see how things could get much worse than they are right now. Besides, I have another assignment elsewhere in the business that I think would be a good fit for Sarah. She could use a change of scene. Give me a week or two to get things settled, and then I am putting you in charge." Then Fred raised his eyebrows and asked, "Now, is there anything you need from me?"

"Well, sir," answered Bobby. "Yes, there is." He took a deep breath. "I don't want to commit to reducing the staff until year-end. I want us to guarantee that anyone who achieves a top level one or level two performance rating (out of five levels of performance the bank used) will not be laid off. I want the department to be given a waiver on the forced ranking system. If everyone achieves a level one rating, then so be it. I'd like to add a cushion over the summer by hiring six science majors from the university across the bay to come in as temporary supervisors. By going after science students, I'll get smart people who seem unlikely to want to make banking their career, and therefore they will not be seen as a threat by the current supervisory team. Lastly, I would like you to encourage all managers in the center to come and cherry pick our best people for promotions into other departments when openings come up."

Fred looked surprised. "You want to lose your best people?"

"Well," answered Bobby. "Obviously that wouldn't be my first choice. But I need to find jobs for sixty people, and the easiest people to place will be my best performers. Besides, I think almost everyone I've met in the department are good, honest, hardworking people."

Fred laughed. "Well, okay. Is there anything else?"

"Oh yes!" answered Bobby. "I would like the internal auditors to stay away for at least three months."

Fred frowned. "Why, are you afraid of oversight?"

"No, not at all. In fact, I would welcome you or any of your team to come in unannounced anytime. We'll put you to work," Bobby answered. "No, the internal auditors would demand too much of my attention, when I need to be focused on the problems and our people.

They would add no value and would be a drain. Plus, they would put out a report before the problems were fixed."

"Okay," Fred replied. "I'll do what I can."

Two weeks later, Bobby found himself standing in front of the 120 people who now reported to him.[46] He explained that they would be reorganizing the work and everyone would be getting a new assignment.

Problem: How to build trust of the people—Starting Point.

> Bobby then explained that by year-end they would be down to sixty people.

> He explained that he'd made an agreement with Fred Schmidt that guaranteed no one who had earned a level one or two performance ranking would be laid off and that he was committed to get everyone into a level one or level two performance rating before any staff reductions would be necessary.

Problem: How to engage the staff—Starting Point.

> Bobby told them that he was committed to placing everyone in a job. He encouraged everyone to try to find

---

46 Sarah Macintosh had been assigned to take a management role in the check processing area. The change of scene was the right thing for Sarah and the bank. She thrived. Her fresh mind allowed her to see opportunities to improve the check processing shop, and she ended up saving the bank $450,000 in annual operating costs in her first year.

a promotion first. Then Bobby told the team that if he had to lay off even a single person, he would lay himself off first. But he said he really needed this job since his wife was expecting their first child in two months. By saying this, he linked his future to every one of them. They were in this together.

Problem: How to empower the staff—Starting Point.

Bobby then told the group that everyone had to get trained in the association rules. He'd put a test up on the PCs in the department that randomly selected twenty-five multiple choice questions from a pool of 100[47]. Everyone must pass this test, and the passing grade was 100 percent. Immediately there was an uproar.

"That's ridiculous. Passing score should be seventy percent," someone said.

"Look, you can take the test as many times as you like. We won't track how many times you take it. You just have to score one hundred percent one time," answered Bobby.

"But, still…one hundred percent!! That's too high."

---

47   In graduate school, as a teaching assistant, Bobby learned the art of writing multiple choice tests. All the answer choices had to be likely good choices, so you really did need to know the material to answer correctly.

"Well," Bobby began. "You can take as long as you like with each attempt, and, it is an open-book test!"

"Maybe, but one hundred percent is still pretty tough," a third person said.

"We'll try it for a week; everyone should try at least twice if they don't get one hundred percent on the first go around. And I'll hand out five sample questions today so you can see what they are like. I think you are all capable of doing this. If necessary, I will sit with you and take a sample test with you. But in the end, each of you must pass this on your own," Bobby said.

It became a contest for some of the staff to study the manuals and score 100 percent on the first try. Several did. Within three weeks, all 120 people had passed the test with 100 percent scores, although several people took the test more than ten times. By the time they finally passed the test, they'd become experts at using the manuals. That was Bobby's objective. He knew the rules changed every six months, and he wanted the staff to know where to find information in the manuals. He wasn't interested in people memorizing the current rules.

More importantly, he wanted them to realize they could take on a tough task and do better than they originally believed they could do. He wanted them to believe in themselves because they were taking on a big challenge.

Problem: How to eliminate the backlog—Staffing

Bobby called the placement office of the university across the bay and ended up with thirty résumés from undergraduates looking for summer work. He asked Illiana, Carlos, Candace, and Florence to look them over and select five each to interview. Several candidates were selected by more than one of the managers, and they ended up interviewing thirteen students. Based on their selection, Bobby hired two chemistry majors, two physics majors, an engineering student, and a math major. They were brought in as temporary supervisors. First, they each had to study and pass the association rules test; at the same time, they were each assigned to rotate through the various jobs to get an understanding of how things currently operated.

Bobby worked with the temporary supervisors and the permanent management team to plan a reorganization of the work.

On the first Friday in June, Bobby called the entire staff together. He announced that on Monday, they would find the entire workplace reorganized. Everyone would have a new job, and if anyone felt he or she needed a fresh start, it would be available.

Over the weekend, the management team, including the temporary supervisors, rearranged the workspace and decorated it with balloons and streamers.

Problem: How to eliminate the backlog—Process

On Monday morning, everyone not in the front end/ back end found himself or herself assigned a new job. Most had responsibility for a single chargeback reason and worked a chargeback desk. Some people had multiple reason codes assigned to their desk because the volume of each was low. In a few cases, more than one person worked the reason code, but the files were distributed to desks so that every chargeback file had an individual with sole responsibility for that file.

Each case by now had a barcode label affixed. As documentation came in, it was distributed to each chargeback desk, where the person responsible for that desk found the correct folder for the documentation.

Everyone assigned to a reason code had the responsibility to clear out the backlog of cases and work toward getting current on the inventory.

In announcing the distribution of people to chargeback desks, Bobby told the staff that they could only guess how productive people could be on different reason codes. "If you feel you are not keeping up and reducing the backlog each day, raise your hand and we will get you help—and it won't cost you anything from a productivity standpoint."

During the first week, a few people did raise their hands. The six supervisors were assigned to help work these desks. At one point, every manager, including Bobby, was sitting side by side with a chargeback expert working cases.

Problem: How to eliminate the backlog—Teamwork

Although the chargeback volume was large, within a single reason code, it could vary greatly week to week. Thus, incoming volume was unpredictable. The first, and most important, measure of productivity was the current nature of the work. Nondocument chargebacks should be completed within ten days. Document chargebacks should be completed within ten days of receiving the documents. In any case, all files needed to be resolved before their time frame expired.

If a chargeback desk was current and had no work to do, the person responsible for the desk could go work on someone else's desk and get credit for that work too. The person who owned the desk would also get credit, since it helped the clerk maintain a current desk.

Initially, HR objected to this measurement method since it could result in two people getting credit for one person's work. Bobby pointed out that success for the bank here was to maintain processing at a current level—thus no losses. Any measurement system that helped the bank achieve that should be encouraged. The HR manager pointed out that double counting could mean several people would achieve an outstanding performance rating. "Look," Bobby pointed out, "the unit has been losing money year in and year out, and we're on track to lose eight million dollars this year. Wouldn't it be outstanding if we could bring the loss rate to zero?"

"Well, of course it would," answered the HR manager.

"And if achieving that outstanding result required the entire team, then wouldn't they all be outstanding performers?"

"Yes, of course," said the HR manager. "But that's not how things are done around here."

"Okay," said Bobby. "But let's see what actually happens and cross that bridge when we come to it."

Within three weeks, a couple of the hardest working of the chargeback desk experts were current on their own desks and had helped others get their desks to current status. One morning, one of the university student supervisors came to Bobby to report that two of the people had traded desks and were working each other's inventory.

Bobby laughed. "Good for them!"

"Won't they each get credit for the other person's work?" asked the student.

"Indeed," answered Bobby. "But look at how much trust it takes to let someone else manage the work for which you're performance is measured. If a file gets screwed up and becomes a loss, it is a huge black mark on the desk. What we are seeing is teamwork and trust. I'll happily give credit for that. Besides, now we have two people who can work either desk!"

The practice spread throughout the unit.

Problem: How to eliminate the backlog with the two airline contracts.

The day after the place was reorganized and decorated with balloons, Fred Schmidt made the trip up from downtown to see how things were going. When Bobby had a few minutes with Fred, he brought up the two airline contracts.

"I've been told that we have contracts written this way because these two airlines are big customers of the commercial section of the bank," Bobby began. "But the way the contracts are structured, with the one-hundred-ten-day clause, we are forced to take losses and have no off-setting revenues. I'd like to suggest that either we renegotiate the contracts or transfer the losses to the commercial section, where presumably they have sufficient revenues to absorb the losses."

Fred Schmidt smiled. "I'd love to see Mark Beeson's face when you suggest that!" (Mark Beeson is the executive vice president for the commercial bank.) "I think you should run the idea up the flagpole and see what they say."

That afternoon Bobby called up Henry Falk, the commercial loan officer responsible for the airline relationships and made his suggestion.

Henry didn't like the idea. "Look," he said, "we don't have a lot of cushion here between our expenses and our revenues. How much are we talking about?"

"Well," answered Bobby, "on one airline, it's running about one point two million dollars per year and on the other it's about two point one million dollars."

"What!" exclaimed Henry. "You've got to be kidding. We have a small deposit from the first airline and no loans, and on the second we have a forty–million-dollar line, but they've never drawn on it. All we get is twenty-five basis points—that's only a hundred thousand per year. There is no way we could ever absorb your losses. By all means, let's renegotiate those contracts."

"Okay," answered Bobby. "Call them today. Under the terms, either party can cancel the contracts immediately. Let's start with that notification."

In the end, the airlines refused to budge, and the bank stopped processing on their behalf. But, during the interim period, the airlines were between a rock and a hard place. While the bank continued to process until the airlines switched to a different processor, the airlines were required to take all disputes that they were responsible for regardless of date. Bobby recovered many losses from the beginning of the year that properly belonged to the airlines.

Problem: How to reduce headcount by sixty people.

Harry Bennet was the HR representative assigned to help Bobby manage the sixty redundant people. Right away, Harry identified six opportunities for promotions for six of the best workers in the chargeback department. Since most of the people had worked in the center for many years, these six workers had long established good reputations and were easy to place into promotions.

When it came to lateral moves, things were slow at first. This was fine with Bobby since he needed the cushion of extra hands as they cleaned up the backlog. A few people found positions and took them.

Things didn't really open up until mid-summer, after the preliminary results of the reorganization were announced. In that meeting, following the announcement of the reorganization's success, one of the managers from the customer service center piped up and said, "We brought in two of Bobby's people. They are amazing. First of all, they know how this business works, and they know the association rules. Second, they are really engaged. It is pretty clear they are respected by their peers. They are hard workers. I wish I had more openings right now because I know where to get good people."

After that endorsement, more people were hired into lateral jobs in the center and eventually elsewhere in the bank. Two of the three MIS people went to work in the data center, and the manager of the MIS group went into the commercial bank.

At the end of November, Bobby put a stop to any further lateral moves. They were down to fifty-eight people. Nobody had been laid off. Bobby reluctantly fired one person. He'd repeatedly shown up unable to work, behaved belligerently, and had refused any treatment for his confessed drug problem.

Two other people asked for early retirement. Bobby worked with Harry in HR to arrange that.

Problem: Eliminate losses.

This was the biggest objective and the easiest to solve.

The reorganization generated trust, engagement, and empowerment in the workforce.

Bobby had recognized the fundamental problem in the prior work organization. By redistributing the files everyday, each clerk had to review each case to determine if it was ready to be worked. Even more damaging was the work measurement. Because the clerks were measured on how many files they completed each day, they would sort them by level of difficulty and work the easy cases first. The hardest cases stayed at the bottom of the pile. Day after day, the hardest cases would remain unworked. Eventually, they became too old to send back to the association and issuer.

The new organization assigned individual cases to individual employees. A tremendous amount of rework was eliminated. The entire quality group's work went away as it was absorbed into the chargeback desks. With ample resources, the individual chargeback desks went from backlogged to current in just over three weeks. The last loss occurred on June 29. As of June 30, the Chargeback Department took not a single dollar of loss for the rest of the year.

Each person was encouraged to look at how his peers organized their work. Each was responsible for choosing a process that worked best for himself. On one occasion, one of the managers sat down with Bobby to complain about how one of the people had organized his desk. Bobby agreed that it sounded like a bad approach but suggested to the manager that the person responsible for the desk should be given a chance to figure it out. Several days later, Bobby spent a good deal of time sitting at this desk asking questions. Bobby never made a suggestion or judgment. Eventually, the person at the desk decided on his own to try a different approach, and things worked out.

When losses went to zero, the team was enormously proud of their accomplishment. Everyone who'd played a role, from Fred Schmidt to the first employee to take a position outside the unit, received a denim shirt with the words Member Chargeback Turnaround Team embroidered on the back. For several years, on the anniversary of the reorganization, these shirts would proudly reappear in various of the bank's departments.

In March of the following year, Fred pulled Bobby off to work another problem area in the bank. Illiana was asked to replace Bobby as department head. By December of that year, the workforce in the Chargeback Department had dropped to thirty-five people, and losses stayed at zero.

BIBLIOGRAPHY

S. Aamodt, S. Wang. Welcome to your Brain. NY: Bloomsbury, 2008.

J.P. Andrew, H.L. Sirkin. Payback: Reaping the Rewards of Innovation. Boston, MA: Harvard Business School Press, 2006.

S.D. Anthony, et al. Creating Breakthrough Innovations. Boston, MA: Harvard Business School Press, (2006)

J.D. Aron. Classics in Software Engineering. Upper Saddle River, NJ: Yourdon Press,1979, 35–39.

F.T. Baker. Chief programmer team management of production programming. IBM Systems Journal, 11, no. 1(1972): 56-73.

R. Bean, R. Radford. The Business of Innovation: Managing the Corporate Imagination for Maximum Results. NY: AMACOM, 2002.

B. Becker, et al. The HR Scorecard. Boston, MA: Harvard Business School Press, 2001.

S. Begley. Train Your Mind Change Your Brain. NY: Ballantine Books, 2007.

S. Berkun. The Myths of Innovation. CA: O'Reilly, Sebastopol, 2007.

D. Bodanis. Electric Universe. NY: Crown Publishers, 2005.

F.P. Brooks. The Mythical Man-Month: Essays on Software Engineering. Addison Wesley Longman, Inc., Boston, (1995) originally (1975)

L.L. Bryan, C.I. Joyce. Mobilizing Minds: Creating Wealth from Talent in the 21st-Century Organization. McGraw-Hill, New York, (2007)

T. Cathcart, D. Klein. Plato and a Platypus walk into a bar...Understanding Philosophy through jokes. Abrams Image, New York, NY, 2007

W.K. Clark. A Time to Lead. Palgrave MacMillan, New York, NY, 2007

J Collins. Good To Great: Why Some Companies Make The Leap...and Others Don't. Harper Collins, New York, 2001

S. Denning. The Secret Language of Leadership. John Wiley & Sons, Inc.,San Francisco, CA, 2007

F.L. Dyer, T.C. Martin. Edison, His Life and Inventions. Harper & Brothers Publishers, New York, MCMX (1910) pp.612

R.P. Feynman, R. Leighton. What Do You Care What Other People Think?: Further Adventures of a Curious Character. W.W. Norton & Company, New York, (1988)

R. Feynman, R. Leighton. Surely You're Joking Mr Feynman! W.W. Norton & Company, New York, 1985

R. Feynman. Perfectly Reasonable Deviations. Basic Books, New York, 2005

J.F. Fixx. More Games for the Super-intelligent. Doubleday & Company, Inc., Garden City, NY, (1976)

J. Frohlichstein. Mathematical Fun, Games and Puzzles. Dover Publication, Inc. New York, (1962)

R.W. Galvin. The Idea of Ideas. Motorola University Press, Schaumburg, IL, 1991

M.J. Gelb, S.M. Caldicott. Innovate Like Edison: The Success System of America's Greatest Inventor. Dutton, NY, (2007)

H. Geneen, B. Bowers. The Synergy Myth: and Other Ailments of Business Today. St. Martin's Press, New York, NY, (1997)

M. Gladwell. The Tipping Point: How Little Things Can Make a Big Difference. Little, Brown and Co., NY, 2000

M. Gladwell. Blink: The Power of Thinking Without Thinking. Little, Brown and Co., New York, NY, 2005

J. Gleick. Genius: The Life and Science of Richard Feynman. Vintage Books, New York, (1992)

M. Gottfredson, S. Schaubert, J. Case, K. Tsakalakis. The Breakthrough Imperative: How the best managers get outstanding results. Collins, New York, NY, 2008

M.B.W. Graham, A.T. Shuldiner. Corning and the Craft of Innovation. Oxford University Press, New York, 2001

E.E. Grant, H. Sackman. An exploratory investigation of programmer performance under on-line and off-line conditions. IEEE Trans. on Human Factors in Electronics, 8(1):33--48, (March 1967)

A. Hartung. Create Marketplace Disruption: How to Stay Ahead of the Competition.. FT Press, New Jersey,, 2008

C. Heath, D. Heath. Made to Stick: Why Some Ideas Survive and Others Die. Random House, New York, NY, (2007)

J. Hipple, S. Wilson, J. Michalski, D. Hardy. Can Corporate Innovation Champions Survive? Chemical Innovation: Vol. 31, No. 11, pp 14-22, November 2001

G. Hofstede, G.J. Hofstede. Cultures and Organizations: Software of the Mind. McGraw-Hill, New York, 2005

M. Hughes. Myers-Briggs Type Indicators and Kirton Adaption-Innovation Inventory Correlations. The Industrial College of the Armed Forces, National Defence University, Washington, D.C.,, 1994

F. Johansson. The Medici Effect: What Elephants and Epidemics Can Teach Us about Innovation. Harvard Business School Press, Boston MA, 2006

J. Kao. Innovation Nation: How America is Losing Its Innvation Edge, Why It Matters, and What We Can Do to Get It Back. Free Press, New York NY, 2007

M. Kawai. Newly-acquired pre-culture behavior of the natural troop of Japanese monkeys on Koshima Islet. Primates, 6, 1-30, 1965

O. Kroeger, J.M. Thuesen, H. Rutledge. Type Talk at Work: How the 16 Personality Types Determine Your Success on the Job. Dell Trade,New York, NY, 2002

T.D. Kuczmarski. Innovation: Leadership Strategies for the Competitive Edge. American Marketing Association,NTC Publishing Group, Chicago, IL,, 1996

A. G. Lafley, R. Charan. The Game-Changer: How you can drive revenue and profit growth with innovation. Crown Business, New York, 2008

D. Landis. The Wealth and Poverty of Nations: Why some are so rich and some so poor.. W.W. Norton & Company, New York, 1998

J. Lehrer. Proust Was a Neuroscientist. Houghton Mifflin Co., Boston, 2007

J. Lehrer. How We Decide. Houghton Mifflin Harcourt Publishing Co., Boston, 2009

P Lencioni. The Five Dysfunctions of a Team. Jossey-Bass, San Francisco, 2002

S. Levitt, S. Dubner. Freconomics: A Rogue Economist Explores the Hidden Side of Everything. HarperCollins Publishers, 2005

R.C. Linger, H.D. Mills,B.I. Witt. Structured Programing: Theory and Practice. Addison Wesley Longman, Inc., Reading, (1979)

F. Maclean. Eastern Approaches. Penguin Books, London, 1949,1991

J.G. March, T. Weil. On Leadership. Blackwell Publishing (English version), 2005

M.E. May. The Elegant Solution: Toyota's Formula for Mastering Innovation. Free Press, New York NY, 2007

J.P. Murmann. Knowledge and Competitive Advantage. Cambridge University Press, Cambridge, UK, 2003

C. O'Reilly, J. Pfeffer. Hidden Value: How Great Companies Achieve Extraordinary Results with Ordinary People.. Harvard Business School Press, Boston MA, 2000

J. Pfeffer, R.I. Sutton. Evidence-Based Management. Harvard Business Review, Decision Making, (2006/01)

D. Pink. A Whole New Mind. Riverhead Books, NY, 2005

C.K. Prahalad, M.S. Krishnan. The New Age of Innovation: Driving Co-Created Value Through Global Networks. McGraw-Hill, New York, 2008

L. Prechelt. An Empirical Comparison of Seven Programming Languages. Computer, Vol 33, No. 10, pp 23-29, (2000)

M. Rayko. Boss: Richard M Daley of Chicago. Signet, New York, (1971)

D. Rushkoff. Get Back in the Box: Innovation from the Inside Out. Collins, New York, NY, 2005

L. Sartain, M.I. Finney. HR from the Heart: Inspiring Stories and Strategies for Building the People Side of Great Business. AMACOM, New York, NY, (2003)

F.L. Schmidt, J.E. Hunter. The Validity and Utility of Selection Methods in Personnel Psychology; Practical and Theoretical Implications of 85 Years of Research Findings. Psychological Bulletin, Vol 124, Iss. 2; Pg 262, (1998/09)

C. Stull, P. Myers, D. Meerman Scott. Tuned In: Uncovering Extraordinary Opportunities That Lead to Business Breakthroughs. John Wiley & Sons, Inc.,Hoboken, New Jersey, 2008

R.I. Sutton. Weird Ideas That Work: How to Build a Creative Company. Free Press, New York NY, (2002)

M. Tomasello, J. Call. Primate Cognition. Oxford University Press, New York, 1997

2-KM Pipe Launched and Submerged at Sidon Pipeline Periscope, Vol. 11 No. 10 Trans-Arabian Pipe Line Company, Beirut, Lebanon, (1963/11)

INDEX

www.ingramcontent.com/pod-product-compliance
Lightning Source LLC
Chambersburg PA
CBHW031833170526
45157CB00001B/288